INTERIOR ARCHITECTURE
DRAFTING AND PERSPECTIVE

INTERIOR ARCHITECTURE
DRAFTING AND PERSPECTIVE

FREDERIC H. JONES, Ph. D.

CRISP. Learning

Menlo Park, California

10   9   8   7   6   5

Printed in the United States of America

Library of Congress Cataloging-in-Publication Data

Jones, Frederic H. (Frederic Hicks), 1944–
  Interior architecture.

  Rev. ed. of: Interior design graphics.
  Bibliography: p.
  1. Architectural drawing—Technique.   2. Interior
architecture—Designs and plans.   3. Perspective.
4. Visual perception.   5. Architectural rendering.
I. Jones, Frederic H. (Frederic Hicks), 1944–
Interior design graphics. II. Title.
NA 2708.J66   1986   729   86-15178
   ISBN 1-56052-092-2

This book is dedicated to Judith, Molly, Mary, Ma and Pa.

CONTENTS

INTRODUCTION

This book is an expanded version of *Interior Design Graphics* which was developed and tested over several years and used with hundreds of students. This version contains fully revised sections from the earlier book, which is still available separately as an inexpensive introduction to basic drafting. *Interior Architecture,* however goes well beyond the scope of the original book, and includes extensive new sections on perception, one and two point perspective and rendering. This additional material is in response to many requests from enthusiastic readers of the earlier book and it attempts to provide a more complete introduction to the world of graphic communication for the growing community of interior architecture students and professionals.

There are many books on drafting and architectural graphics. None of them, however, presents a simple explanation of design for the absolute beginner. Another important omission in those books is a representative set of examples of professional drafting and rendering with which the students and other professionals can compare their work and ideas. This comparison of notes is one of the best teaching methods. Finally, most texts do not present standards. While it is impossible to be comprehensive in a book of this size, I have provided a significant compilation of standards as well as references to enable you to research and add to your own standards collection.

I hope this new book will not only expand the utility of its predecessor as a basic drafting and drawing text but that it will also be useful to students and professional designers as both a reference text of standards and examples, and a source of ideas and information.

TOOLS

Tools are more than tools! They are a romantic symbol of what we do and how we do it. Tools are a badge of our profession. I cannot stress too much the importance of appropriate and quality tools. On the other hand, tools need not be the most expensive available. Moderately priced and well-made tools are available and can be as effective and satisfying as the gold plated, engraved, presentation variety.

I have outlined here the basic tools you will encounter as an interior design draftsman, as well as many optional ones. Become familiar with the field and keep your eye out in the art supply store for new products. You will find, if you are like me, that you will acquire a collection of tools that will be occasionally useful, and a few treasured favorites which will be your mainstays. My favorite red drafting pencil and a tinted, 3" adjustable triangle go with me like Linus' blanket.

A sturdy drafting board, either a lap or table type, is necessary for serious drafting. A metal edge is required if a t-square is to be used. The surface should be covered with a drafting cover such as *Borco* plastic for maximum utility. The surface should never be cut on or punctured with tacks. Only drafting tape is acceptable for fastening drawings. The board should be larger than the largest sheet of paper you expect to use. A typical board size for interior design drawing is 30" x 42".

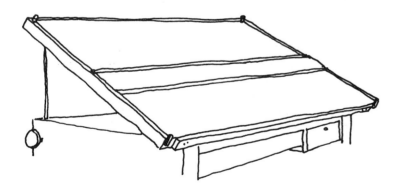

The parallel edge such as *Mayline* or *Paradraft* is mounted with cable on the drawing board. It moves smothly up and down, remaining parallel, but without the hand tension required of the t-square. This is much preferred over the t-square for serious drafters. The kind you mount yourself on top of the board is much smoother than the one that comes integrated with the board by the factory. It is simple to install yourself.

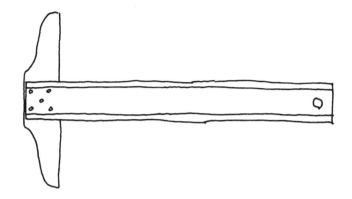

The t-square is used to draw lines parallel to the drawing board front edge. It is snuggled tightly against the drawing board edge and the pencil is drawn across the plastic edge to make a straight and parallel line. Angled and perpendicular lines are constructed with a triangle. A wooden t-square with a clear plastic edge is the preferred one for drafting.

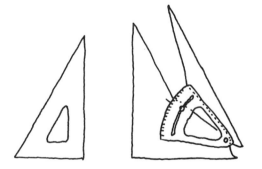

Triangles are used for drawing lines other than horizontal. They are standard in 45º, 30º/60º, and adjustable in many sizes. The adjustable is the basic tool and an 8" triangle would be a good first choice. A large 12" 45º triangle would be a good choice for long lines. A 3" 30º/60º is good for hatching and lettering.

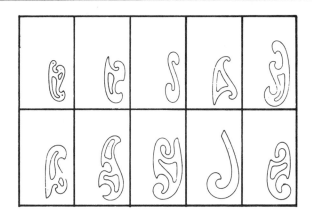

French curves are used to draw curved segments of objects or plans. They are drawn against with pencil or pen after an appropriate segment is selected. A selection of two or three is usually enough for interior design drafting.

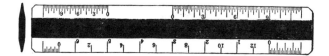

Scale rules come in triangular and flat styles, and in 6" and 12" lengths. 1/4" scale means that a foot in the actual building would be represented by 1/4" on the plan. The scale rule makes thinking in scale much easier, for in the 1/4" scale, the rule is marked just as if each 1/4" is a foot, and these "small" feet are   broken into 12 "inches." Other scales like 1/8", 1/4", 1/2", 3/8", 1-1/2", and 3" are represented. A 12" triangular scale rule is the basic scale rule.

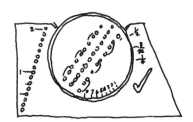

A lettering guide is used to make light pencil guidelines to assure neat and uniform lettering on plans and drawings. This is used with hand lettering, not templates. Instructions for its use come with the device.

The lead holder with loose lead is superior to wood-clad pencils for drafting. It can hold any hardness of lead, and can quickly be changed and sharpened with the lead pointer. "F" lead is standard for all-around drafting.

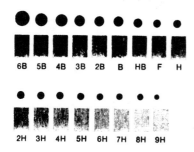

6B 5B 4B 3B 2B B HB F H

2H 3H 4H 5H 6H 7H 8H 9H

Graphite (black) drawing pencil: The term "lead" pencil is a misnomer. The principal ingredient of most drawing pencils is graphite, a black mineral variety of carbon. The degree of hardness is indicated by a standard code; this chart approximates diameters of 17 degrees.

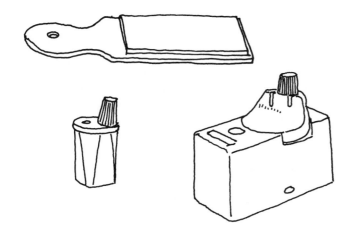

The pencil pointer is as basic as the pencil holder and lead to the drafter. The basic type with steel cutter is recommended over other types. It has several bushings for different pencil diameters, and has a gauge for blunt or sharp cutting. A sand-paper board is good for rendering and sketching. It can chisel and blunt leads for special techniques.

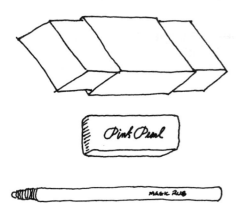

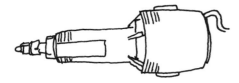

The *Magic Rub* and *Pink Pearl* are the basic erasers for drafting and come in pencil, block or plug form for electric erasers.

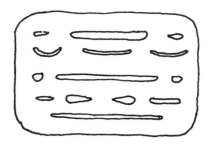

The electric eraser is a basic tool of the drafter, and comes in both cord and cordless types. It saves time and makes a much neater tracing than conventional erasers.

A stainless steel eraser shield is used to mask off parts of the drawing you don't want to erase, and to expose those you do. Just lay it over the pencil mark with the error exposed through an opening, and erase. The steel part protects the good line and makes a much neater correction.

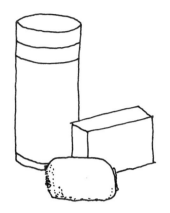

Dry cleaning pad is sprinkled on the tracing as the drafter works. It keeps the tracing clean of graphite smudges. It is best not to rub it on the paper. The material is similar to eraser dust, and absorbs the loose graphite dust that can smudge your paper.

Leroy Lettering Sets use a plastic template to guide a scriber with an ink pen to letter many sizes and styles of type on plans and drawings. This is an excellent way for neat titles. Sets come with as few as three lettering templates and a scribe.

Drafting tape is not as sticky as masking tape, and is used to hold tracing paper to the drafting board without damaging the paper or the drawing surface. Drafting tape is also less likely to leave gum on the paper and drafting board. 3/4" wide tape is the best all-around size.

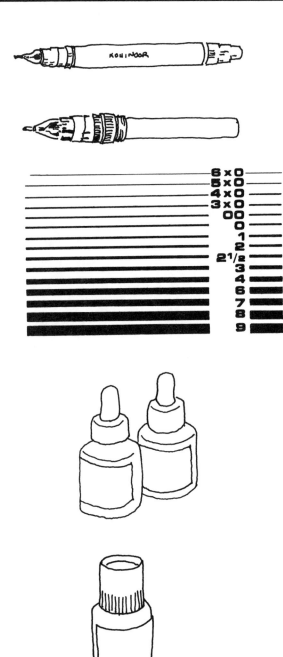

The technical pen is the basic ink drawing instrument. It is easy to use and comes in many line widths for various needs. It produces a uniform line width. A good basic set would include a 00 (very fine), 0, 2 1/2; then add 000, 1, 2, and 4. 00 is a good sketching instrument to use when you occasionally need to draft lines in ink for presentations and the like.

Colored drawing ink, one of the most versatile mediums, is used for many purposes. It comes in two basic types: translucent and opaque. Black india ink (waterproof) is opaque and best for working drawings, fine line work and washes. It is free from dye and contains carbon as a pigment. Special inks (like "acetate" ink) are made for use on water repellent drafting surfaces, such as acetate, *Mylar* film, *Lumarith*, tracing cloth and similar plastic materials, without "crawling."

Drawing inks have a reasonable degree of permanence if kept from sunlight or strong diffused light. Shellac is the usual water-proofing ingredient--therefore it is necessary to thoroughly clean pens, instruments and brushes after use. Several pen cleaners listed are good for this purpose.

To dilute black ink, add pure water with four drops of aqual ammonia to the ounce. Tap water will suffice for washes which are applied at once. To dilute colored inks, use pure water only. Never add any acid or mix ink brands.

A drafting brush is ideal for dusting erasure leavings and graphite dust off your tracings and board.

A flexible curve can take the place of French Curves, and at the same time allow you to customize your own shapes. It also allows you to transfer a shape from one drawing to another.

A good drafting board lamp is mandatory. One that gives good strong light with an opaque shade that prevents direct glare is best. Also, a flexible one that can move about to prevent reflected glare is important.

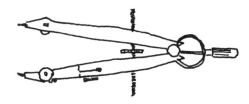

A Bow compass is handy for drawing circles and arcs. This can substitute for a circle template, and will work with both pencil and ink.

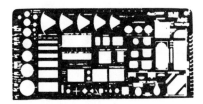

ABC

Scale 1/8"
Door swings, circles, etc.

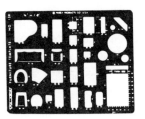

FURNITURE

Scale 1/4"   Size 5-1/4" x 6-3/4"
For quickly visualizing furniture space and adaptability, 65 pieces
of furniture and width, depth and height of each.

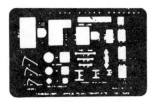

OFFICE PLAN

Office equipment at 1/4" scale.
Size: 4-1/2" x 7".

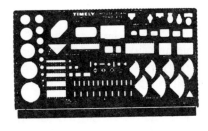

HOUSE PLAN

Scale 1/4" Size 4-7/8" x 6-3/4"
Door swings, circles, etc.

PAPER

BASIC PAPER TERMS

TOOTH is the arrangement of fibers in the surfaces of paper which form little peaks or depressions referred to as "teeth." Created by an unevenness of surface in the manufacture, these peaks actually appear from the depression of the pencil, lead, crayon or pastel. More toothing makes for a rougher surface..bulkier and more absorbent. There is also more light reflection as the tooth increases. The term "bite" is also often used to describe this textured result.

FEEL is used to express the reaction to physically handling a paper; its comparative bulk, resiliency, finish, "snap," weight, etc.

GRAIN is the direction the fibers of a paper run as it is manufactured. It affects surface, directional patterns, folding, tear qualities and dimensionable stability.

HARD is used to describe high finish but really indicates a high degree of water resistance imparted by surface sizing.

SLICK is used to express a smooth vellum-like finish, usually stated as "high" or "plate" finish.

LB. SUBSTANCE refers to the weight of a paper in pounds. The lb. designation of a paper is determined by the weight of a ream (500 sheets) in its basic size. For example: the basic size of bond papers is 17" x 22". 500 sheets of a light weight bond in this size would weigh 16 pounds...hence, 16-lb. paper. 500 sheets of a ledger bond (heavier weight) in this size would weigh 32 pounds...hence, 32-pound paper. The basic sizes of papers vary from grade to grade, arbitrarily dictated by paper mills many years ago to accommodate the sizes of printing presses.

RAG CONTENT indicates that a paper contains a percentage of rag or cotton pulp, from 25% to 100%. The richness and permanence of a sheet varies with the percentage of the rag content, and makes for better erasability.

BRISTOL BOARD SURFACES

HIGH SURFACE (Smooth or Plate Finish). A uniformly smooth finish
overall; takes the most delicate line techniques in pen or pencil.

MEDIUM SURFACE (Kid or Vellum Finish). A "toothy," slightly textured finish for almost any technique: line and wash, air brush, tempera, acrylic, pastel, etc.

Either surface withstands repeated erasures and reworking without feathering.

ILLUSTRATION,   MAT,   MOUNT   BOARD   AND   PAPER THICKNESSES

ST Single Thick (Appx. 1/16" or 60 pts.)
DT Double Thick (Appx. 1/8" or 110 pts.)
TT Triple Thick (Appx. 3/16" or 165 pts.)

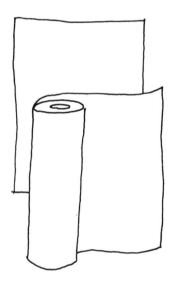

BOND PAPER 16-lb. is approximately .003 points thick.

LEDGER PAPER 32-lb. is approximately .006 points thick.

PAPER QUANTITIES

QUIRE: 25 sheets
REAM: 500 sheets

DRAFTING PAPER: Two kinds are used extensively in interior design drafting. The first is roll tracing paper that comes in white and yellow, and in various widths--18" is recommended. This is inexpensive and is used for under- and over-lays, layouts and sketching. The second type is 16 or 20 lb., 100% rag drafting vellum for finished work. This comes in plain and pre-boardered in many sizes--18" x 24" and 24" x 30" are the most common. The most popular brands are *Clearprint #1000*, *Albanene* and *Teledine Natural*. The pre-bordered kind with end titleblocks are the most common for architecture and interior design. The type with the blue grids is most commonly used for engineering. It is usually divided into 10ths or 8ths.

PAPER FINISHES

These listings are intended for quick reference purposes, and include the most common words used in the art materials field. Consider these terms as a general guide. There are other words (of more specialized usage) that are used to describe finishes.

SMOOTH Usually described by the following terms:

Clay	Plate
Glazed	Smooth
High	Super
Hot Press	Super Calendered

MEDIUM Usually described by the following terms:

Cold Press	Regular
Dull	Satin
Eggshell	Slightly Grained
Kid	Unglazed
Matte	Vellum
Medium	Velour
Parchment	

ROUGH Usually described by the following terms:

Antique	Irregular
Coarse	Laid
Cockle	Machine
Embossed	Rough
Felt	

MUSEUM (RAG) BOARD

A specially formulated board used primarily by conservators, professional picture framers and others who are concerned about the longevity of works of art. It is acid-free (pH) neutral; usually made in white or off-white. Neither acidic nor alkaline, museum board does not contain chemicals which will stain the art by contact. It is suggested that this board be used for the mounting and framing of original lithographs and historic or valuable documents.

BLUEPRINTING

"Blueprinting" is a process of inexpensively reproducing an original drawing. This process allows the designer, who draws plans, details and other types of drawings on transparent or translucent paper, to have one or one-hundred copies to give to the client and contractors, and still protect the valuable original.

In times past, architects paid people to make "tracings" of their original drawings to give to the contractors. This process was supplanted by the "blueprinting" process and left us with the term "tracing" which is still used to describe that original drawing on translucent paper. The "blueprinting" process itself has since been largely replaced by a much more inexpensive process called *Diazo*.

Diazo is a positive-to-posivite process, rather than a positive- to-negative one like "blueprinting." It is a relatively dry process. Special machines are used to expose the "tracing" and a sensitive paper to ultra violet light. Then the sensitive copy is developed into a final copy. These *Diazo* copies come in blue line, brown and black line prints on bond paper, heavy "presentation" paper, or vellum (called Sepias). *Mylar* prints are also available. The prints are usually made on a white background. The clarity of the background depends on a high contrast between the lines drawn on the tracing and the vellum on which it is drawn. This is the reason you should make clear and dark lines in your original. Very light lettering guidelines and light blue colored pencil lines are virtually invisible to the *Diazo* machine and can be ignored when you prepare your tracing for reproduction.

It is important that you understand this reproduction process for it is the standard one for which you will prepare your originals. It is useful to visit a local graphics reproduction company and ask them to show you all their "tricks."

Another process that will become useful as you become more adept is Xerox 2080 enlargement or reduction of your drawings. Details may also be Xeroxed or printed on stick-back plastic and placed on your drawing. This replaces repeated tracings of a standard detail from sheet to sheet.

It is also important to note that the "Sepia" copies, as well as the *Xerox 2080* copies on vellum, can serve as the base of additional tracings and *Diazo* reproductions, for these "second originals" are indistinguishable from the "first originals."   They may also be erased! I always make a Base plan, then make several "Sepia" second originals that become the ground on which to lay out the Reflected Ceiling, Furniture, Electrical, and other sheets. This means that much of the work is done by the blueprint company, and I don't have to trace the walls over and over again. The cost is very reasonable when compared to your hourly fee!

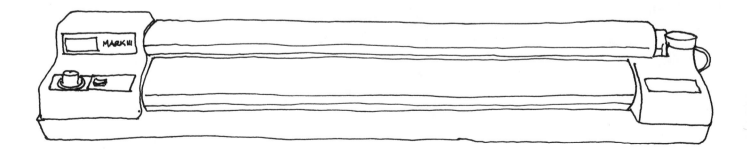

SYMBOLS

λ represents man in Chinese characters. "3" can stand for ⌣⌣⌣ . ⌐⊙⊙⌐ is obviously an automobile, though very simplified. All these are examples of symbols shich we come to recognize as second nature. The symbols of architectural drawing are similar. They are simplifications of the way something would actually look, but with only the essential details, like the automobile drawing above. Here are some examples of plan symbols.

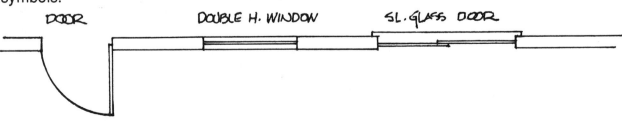

DOOR   DOUBLE H. WINDOW   SL. GLASS DOOR

SCALE

Even with the simplification of these symbols, it would be both difficult and expensive to draw a plan at full size, besides requiring quite a drawing board and t-square! So designers and architects have elected to "scale" down the drawing by substituting a smaller measurement for a larger one. For example, 1/8" instead of 1 foot, or 1 centimeter instead of 1 meter. This is written: 1/4" = 1'-0". 1/4", 1/8", and 1/2" are common scales in interior design, but others are sometimes used as well. To aid in converting to scales easily and with accuracy, a scale ruler is used.

To use the scale rule, place the ruler using whichever scale is indicated (usually 1/4"). Center the zero on the scale on one of the points you are measuring, and read the footage at the other point. If it reads between two foot dimensions, (i.e., 24 or 25), move the smaller dimension to the second point, and now the zero will be off the first mark. Notice that to the outside of the zero there are smaller marks. These indicate inches and fractions of inches. If you add the inches between the zero and the mark, of the foot dimension over the second mark, you will have the scale dimension (i.e., 24' 6-1/2").

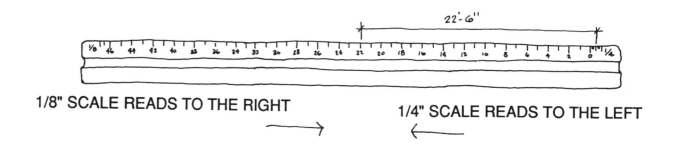

1/8" SCALE READS TO THE RIGHT

1/4" SCALE READS TO THE LEFT

FURNITURE TEMPLATES

ROUND COCKTAIL TABLE

DIAMETEER	HEIGHT
24"	16"
30"	15"
36"	16"
42"	15"
48"	16"

CORNER TABLE

WIDTH	DEPTH	HEIGHT
28"	28"	20"
30"	30"	15"

BUNCHING TABLE

WIDTH	DEPTH	HEIGHT
20"	20"	15"
19"	19"	15"
21"	21"	16"

COCKTAIL TABLE

WIDTH	DEPTH	HEIGHT
35"	19"	17"
50"	18"	15"
54"	20"	15"
56"	21"	16"
57"	19"	15"
58"	20"	15"
61"	21"	17"

END TABLE

WIDTH	DEPTH	HEIGHT
21"	28"	20"
22"	28"	21"
26"	20"	21"
27"	19"	22"
28"	28"	20"

OTTOMAN

WIDTH	DEPTH	HEIGHT
22"	18"	13"
22"	22"	16"
24"	19"	16"

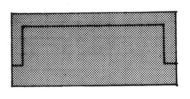

SOFA

WIDTH	DEPTH	HEIGHT
72"	36"	28"
76"	35"	35"
84"	36"	37"
87"	31"	31"
88"	32"	29"
91"	32"	30"

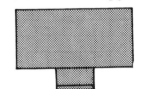

DESK

WIDTH	DEPTH	HEIGHT
50"	21"	30"
50"	22"	30"
55"	26"	29"
60"	30"	29"
72"	36"	29"

SMALL ARM CHAIR

WIDTH	DEPTH	HEIGHT
18"	18"	29"
21"	22"	32"

FURNITURE TEMPLATE

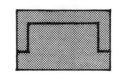

LOVE SEAT

WIDTH	DEPTH	HEIGHT
47"	28"	36"
54"	30"	36"
59"	36"	37"

ROUND COMMODE

DIAMETER	HEIGHT
18"	20"
24"	20"
26"	20"

STEP TABLE

WIDTH	DEPTH	HEIGHT
15"	27"	21"
19"	30"	21"
20"	30"	23"

SOFA TABLE

WIDTH	DEPTH	HEIGHT
48"	16"	29"
44"	26"	30"

HEXAGONAL COMMODE

WIDTH	DEPTH	HEIGHT
27"	27"	20"
28"	28"	22"

SQUARE COMMODE

WIDTH	DEPTH	HEIGHT
24"	24"	20"
25"	25"	21"
26"	26"	20"
26"	26"	21"

SHELF UNITS

WIDTH	DEPTH	HEIGHT
17"	10"	60"
24"	10"	60"
36"	10"	36"
36"	10"	60"
48"	10"	60"

CONSOLE TELEVISION

WIDTH	DEPTH	HEIGHT
37"	17"	29"
38"	17"	29"
40"	18"	30"
45"	18"	30"
47"	19"	30"

RECTANGULAR COMMODE

WIDTH	DEPTH	HEIGHT
18"	24"	20"
22"	28"	20"

FURNITURE TEMPLATE

SERVER OR CART

LENGTH	WIDTH	HEIGHT
36"	16"	30"
52"	18"	33"
64"	16"	30"

DINING CHAIRS

WIDTH	DEPTH	HEIGHT
17"	19"	29"
20"	17"	36"
22"	19"	29"
24"	21"	31"

SEAT HEIGHT 16"

BUFFET

LENGTH	WIDTH	HEIGHT
36"	16"	31"
48"	16"	31"
52"	18"	31"

ROUND DINING TABLE

DIAMETER	HEIGHT
32"	28"
36"	28"
42"	28"
48"	28"

CHINA CABINET OR HUTCH

LENGTH	WIDTH	HEIGHT
48"	16"	65"
50"	20"	60"
62"	16"	66"

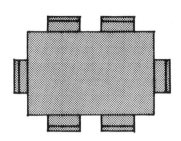

RECTANGULAR DINING TABLE

LENGTH	WIDTH	HEIGHT
42"	30"	29"
48"	30"	29"
48"	42"	29"
60"	40"	28"
60"	42"	29"
72"	36"	28"

OVAL DINING TABLE

LENGTH	WIDTH	HEIGHT
54"	42"	28"
60"	42"	28"
72"	40"	28"
72"	48"	28"
84"	42"	28"

FURNITURE TEMPLATE

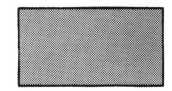

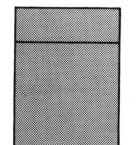

DRESSER

WIDTH	DEPTH	HEIGHT
48"	18"	30"
50"	18"	30"
52"	16"	30"
60"	18"	30"

DOUBLE BED

	LENGTH	WIDTH
Double Bed	75"	54"
	80"	54"
	84"	54"
Queen-Size Bed	80"	60"
	84"	60"
King-Size Bed	80"	72"
	80"	76"
	84"	72"
	84"	76"

SINGLE BED

	LENGTH	WIDTH
Bunk Bed	75"	30"
	75"	33"
Dormitory Bed	75"	33"
	80"	36"
Twin Bed	75"	39"
	80"	36"
Twin Bed	75"	39"
	80"	39"
	84"	39"
Three Qtr. Bed	75"	48"
	80"	48"

NIGHT TABLE

LENGTH	WIDTH	HEIGHT
24"	15"	22"
22"	16"	22"
24"	18"	22"
22"	22"	22"

CHEST OF DRAWERS

WIDTH	DEPTH	HEIGHT
20"	16"	50"
26"	16"	37"
28"	15"	34"
32"	17"	43"
36"	18"	45"

DESK

WIDTH	DEPTH	HEIGHT
33"	16"	29"
36"	16"	29"
40"	20"	30"
43"	16"	30"

KITCHEN TEMPLATE

RANGE HOOD

WIDTH	HEIGHT	DEPTH
24"	5"	12"
30"	6"	17"
66"	7"	26"
72"	8"	28"

BUILT-IN COOK TOP

WIDTH	HEIGHT	DEPTH
12"	2"	18"
24"	3"	22"
48"	3"	22"

REFERIGERATOR

CU.FT.	WIDTH	HEIGHT	DEPTH
9	24"	56"	29"
12	30"	68"	30"
14	31"	63"	24"
19	34"	70"	29"
21	36"	66"	29"

SINGLE COMPARTMENT SINK

WIDTH	DEPTH
24"	21"
30"	20"

DOUBLE COMPARTMENT SINK

WIDTH	DEPTH
32"	21"
36"	20"
42"	21"

STANDARD FREE-STANDING RANGE

WIDTH	HEIGHT	DEPTH
20"	30"	24"
21"	36"	25"
30"	36"	26"
40"	36"	27"

DROP-IN RANGE

WIDTH	HEIGHT	DEPTH
23"	23"	22"
24"	23"	22"
30"	24"	25"

OFFICE SEATING TEMPLATE

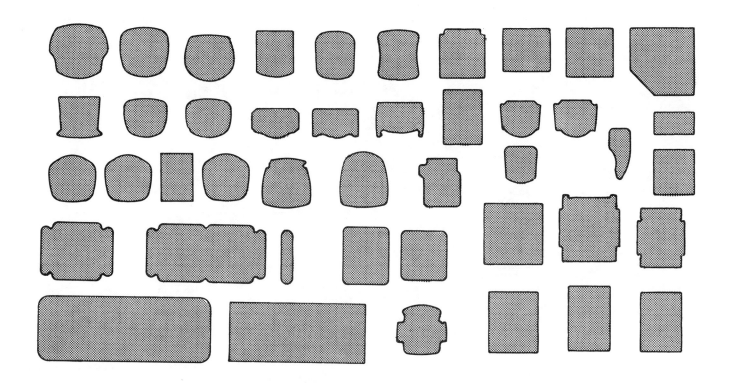

SCALE 1/4″–1 0″

OFFICE FURNITURE TEMPLATE

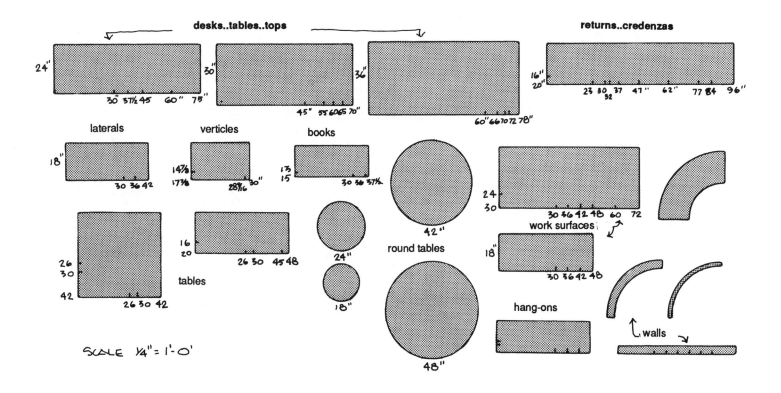

desks..tables..tops

returns..credenzas

24"   30   36"

30 37½ 45   60" 75"

45" 55 60 65 70"

60" 66 70 72 78"

16"
20"   23 30 37   47"   62"   77 84   96"
       32

laterals   verticles   books

18"   14⅞   13   24
       17⅞   15   30

30 36 42   28⁷⁄₁₆ 30"   30 36 37½

42"

30 36 42 48 60 72

16
20   26 30 45 48

24"   round tables   work surfaces

18"   30 36 42 48

26
30   18"
42   26 30 42

tables   48"   hang-ons

walls

SCALE ¼"= 1'-0'

RESTAURANT FURNITURE TEMPLATE

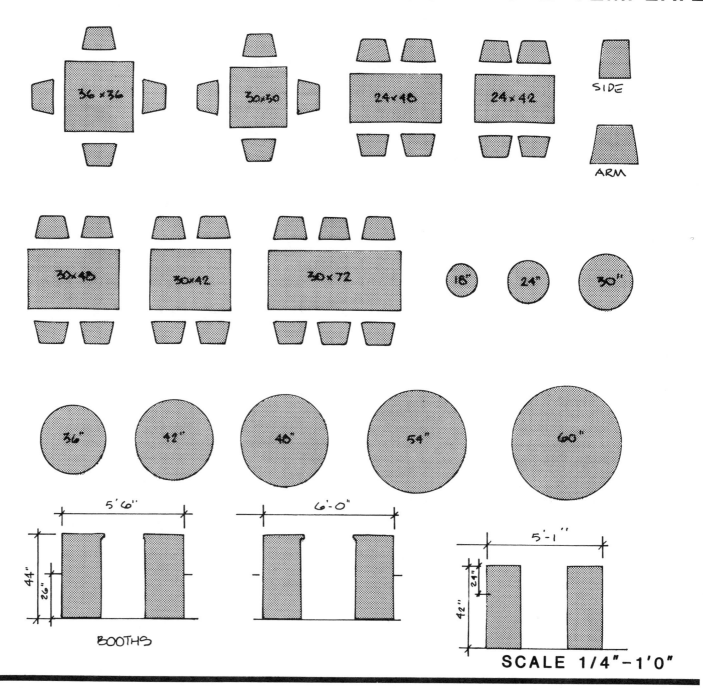

36 x 36   30 x 30   24 x 48   24 x 42   SIDE

ARM

30 x 48   30 x 42   30 x 72   18"   24"   30"

36"   42"   48"   54"   60"

5'6"   6'0"   5'1"

44"   26"   24"   42"

BOOTHS   SCALE 1/4"-1'0"

ELECTRICAL SYMBOLS

CEILING OUTLET FIXTURE	SINGLE RECEPTACLE OUTLET	SINGLE-POLE SWITCH
RECESSED OUTLET FIXTURE	DUPLEX RECEPTACLE OUTLET	DOUBLE-POLE SWITCH
DROP CORD FIXTURE	TRIPLEX RECEPTACLE OUTLET	THREE-WAY SWITCH
FAN HANGER OUTLET	QUADRUPLEX RECEPTACLE OUTLET	FOUR-WAY SWITCH
JUNCTION BOX	SPLIT-WIRED DUPLEX RECEPTACLE OUTLET	WEATHERPROOF SWITCH
FLUORESCENT FIXTURE	SPECIAL PURPOSE SINGLE RECEPTACLE OUTLET	LOW VOLTAGE SWITCH
TELEPHONE	230 VOLT OUTLET	PUSH-BUTTON
INTERCOM	WEATHERPROOF DUPLEX OUTLET	CHIMES
CEILING FIXTURE WITH PULL SWITCH	DUPLEX RECEPTACLE WITH SWITCH	TELEVISION ANTENNA OUTLET
SPECIAL FIXTURE OUTLET	SPECIAL DUPLEX OUTLET	DIMMER SWITCH
THERMOSTAT	FLUSH MOUNTED PANEL BOX	SPECIAL SWITCH

PLUMBING SYMBOLS

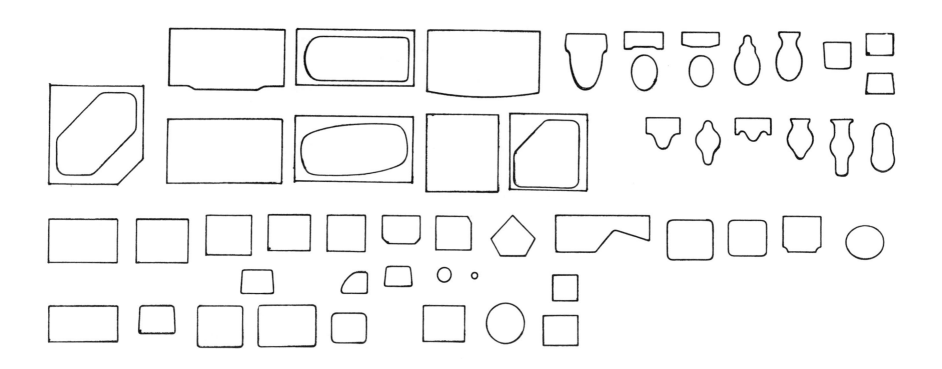

SCALE 1/4" –1'0"

ARCHITECTURAL SYMBOLS

ELEV.   SECTION
    CONCRETE

ELEV.   SEC.   PLAN
        BLOCK

ELEV.   SEC.   PLAN
    BRICK

SEC.   GLASS
EARTH

ELEV.   SEC.   PLAN   MARBLE
    WOOD

JOB NAME _____

LOCATION _____

DATE _____

RESIDENTIAL WINDOW REPLACEMENT
FIELD MEASUREMENT GUIDE
for Wood Frame and Brick Veneer Construction

Existing exterior:

____ Good; not to be disturbed.

____ New siding to be installed.

____ New siding recently installed.

____ Brick veneer.

*If exterior wood trim is to be covered, give trim width dimensions in column **F** below.

Existing interior:

____ Good; not to be disturbed.

____ To be remodeled.

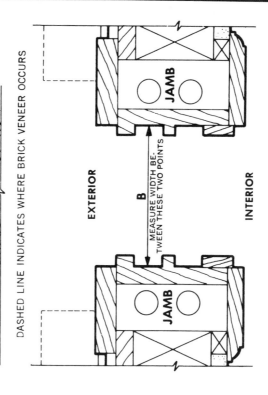

MEASURE HEIGHT BETWEEN THESE TWO POINTS

HEAD

SILL

INTERIOR

EXTERIOR

A

C

D

DASHED LINE INDICATES WHERE BRICK VENEER OCCURS

JAMB

JAMB

EXTERIOR

INTERIOR

B

MEASURE WIDTH BETWEEN THESE TWO POINTS

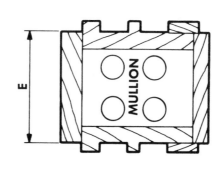

MULLION

E

AS19–479

LOCATION	A	B	C	D	E	F*	QTY.	PELLA UNIT SIZE	PRICE

ROLSCREEN COMPANY • PELLA, IOWA 50219

WINDOW SYMBOLS

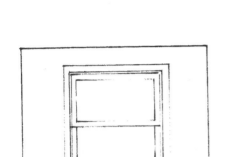

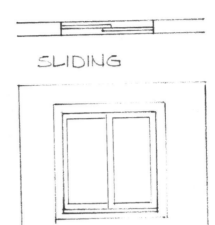

SLIDING

DOUBLE HUNG

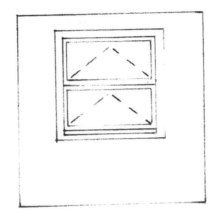

AWNING

IN MASONRY

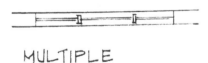

MULTIPLE

PICTURE

CASEMENT

Pella WOOD DOUBLE-HUNG WINDOWS

Scale 3″ = 1′ 0″ (1:4)

FRAME — DRYWALL

¾″ (19) Sheathing   ½″ (13) Drywall

2 x 6 FRAME — DRYWALL

¾″ (19) Sheathing   ½″ (13) Drywall

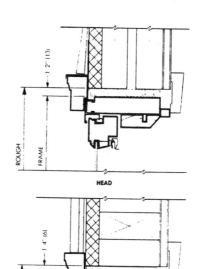

HEAD

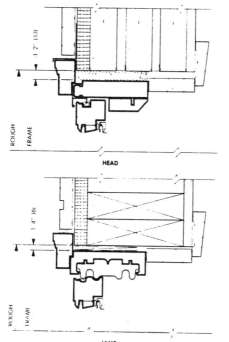

HEAD

JAMB

JAMB

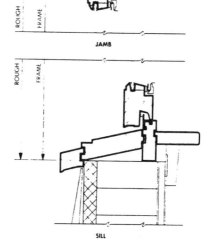

SILL

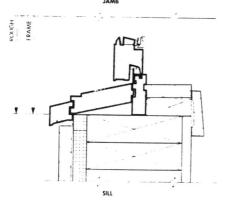

SILL

DOOR SYMBOLS

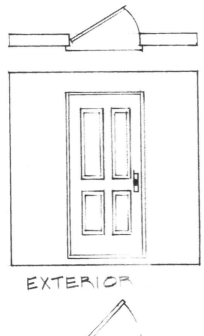

EXTERIOR

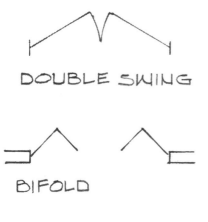

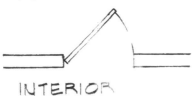

INTERIOR

ACCORDIAN

DOUBLE SWING

BIFOLD

POCKET

CASED OPENING

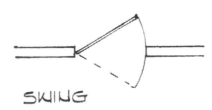

SWING

Pella WOOD SLIDING GLASS DOORS

Scale 3″ = 1′ 0″ (1:4)

5

FRAME — DRYWALL   **2 x 6 FRAME — DRYWALL**

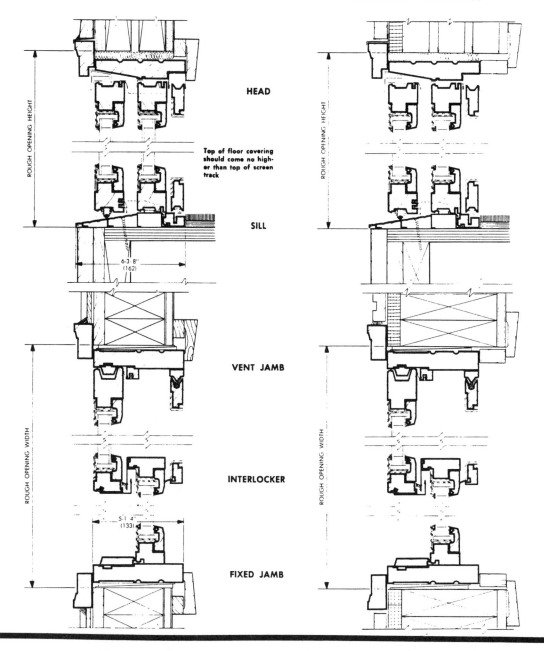

ROUGH OPENING HEIGHT

HEAD

Top of floor covering should come no higher than top of screen track

SILL

6-3·8″
(162)

VENT JAMB

ROUGH OPENING WIDTH

INTERLOCKER

5-1·4″
(133)

FIXED JAMB

TECHNIQUES

In architectural drafting the line is the primary symbol used to convey space, shape, even texture. Scale and relationship are communicated by placement and dominance of lines. Lines also have certain symbolic qualities expressed in line types. Line quality communicates clarity and professionalism.

When drafting, always know what a line represents. Draw enough, but no more than necessary, to convey your meaning. Knowing and communicating clearly the construction of a cabinet is far more important than line quality, but that too is important. Make sure corners connect and that all lines are logical and contiguous with meaning.

Most architectural drafting is done on paper with pencil, but ink and plastic film also have their uses. We will, however, concentrate on pencil drawn on paper because of its flexibility and correctability.

A good set of tools will work for your drafting quality. A drafting board larger than the paper you propose to use is important. A drafting board 28" x 42" is a good architectural size, allowing for the use of 24" x 36" paper. A good plastic surface for the drafting board is best. A parallel straight edge is much better than a t-square, and is more suitable for drawing long, straight lines in architectural drafting. An adjustable triangle, a drafting pencil and sharpener, a scale rule, and an eraser round out the list of basic tools. These and other items are covered in the tool section of this book.

Mount your paper, usually Clear Print or other architectural vellum, to the board. Align the paper edge with the parallel bar. This will assure the accuracy of the lines, and expedite removing and repositioning the paper as you work on it. Tape the paper to the board only at the corners, using drafting tape which will allow the paper to stretch without bubbling.

MAJOR LINES, the outer major elements of a plan, elevation or section, or cut lines should be the boldest. HB or F lead is indicated.

SECONDARY LINES are for internal and subordinate lines, including dimension lines. These should be as dark as major lines, but not quite so dominant. HB or F lead is also good for these lines.

LAYOUT LINES are faint, and may be done with F lead or a harder grade. These lines are intended to be unseen or faintly seen. This line weight is also indicated for lettering guides.

LINE TYPES:

———————— Solid line for major and secondary elements

- - - - - - - - - -   Dashed line for elements above and below cut lines of plan

-.-.-.-.-.-.-.-.-   Center lines

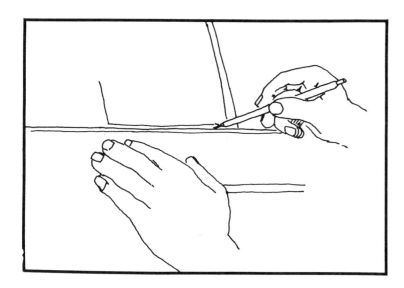

Always draw over the t-square and triangle and other tool edges, not into them. There should be a slight gap between the lead tip and the plastic tool edge. This protects the tool edge, makes it easier to see the line, and reduces smudging. Pull the pencil rather than pushing it, as this keeps the paper from snagging.

Keep the lead sharp. About every 12" to 18" of line drawn will require you to sharpen. As dark a line as you can make is the one to aim for at the beginning, but thin and not fuzzy.

To help assure the evenness of a drafting line, rotate the pencil while drawing.

Make your corners clean. Avoid double lines when drawing on existing lines. If this occurs, erase both and redraw them. All lines should start and end with clarity and definition. Don't let lines fade away.

LETTERING

There is no single element more important in interior architectural drafting than lettering. This element makes the most difference in the professional look of plans and details. There are many styles of lettering and many mechanical aids for lettering, but for most notes, dimensions and details, there is no substitute for freehand lettering.

For large scale titles and formal presentation boards, Paratype, *Kroy* Lettering templates, *Leroy* Machines and others are acceptable. See the tool section for information on these systems.

Lettering should be neat and in scale with the drawings it is illuminating. You must train your eye along good design principles, as well as your hand. A sharp pencil and the lettering guide are used to make light consistent guide lines to letter within. If you have troble getting the lines light enough with the "F" lead, use a 2H or 4H lead for the guidelines only. The resultant guidelines are left on the drawing and become part of the texture. Very little of the guidelines will show through when tracings are blueprinted.

A 2" or 3" triangle can be useful in judging the consistency of the verticle lines of your letters. It need not be used to draw against. Its use is to guide the eye.

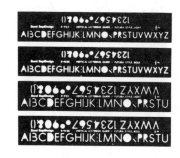

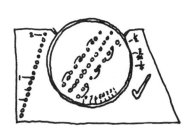

ELEVATION ELEVATION ELEVATION GROUND
ELEVATION ELEVATION BASEMENT GROUND
BASEMENT BASEMENT BASEMENT GROUND
BASEMENT SOUTH SOUTH SOUTH SOUTH
SOUTH EAST EAST EAST EAST EAST WEST
WEST WEST WEST WEST NORTH NORTH
NORTH NORTH NORTH FIRST FIRST FIRST
FIRST FIRST FLOOR FLOOR FLOOR FLOOR
FLOOR SECOND SECOND SECOND SECOND
SECOND THIRD THIRD THIRD THIRD THIRD
FOURTH FOURTH FOURTH FOURTH FOURTH
GROUND GROUND GROUND GROUND FLOOR
GROUND GROUND GROUND GROUND FLOOR
GROUND GROUND GROUND GROUND FLOOR
FLOOR FLOOR SECTION SECTION SECTION
SECTION SECTION PLAN PLAN PLAN PLAN
PLAN SITE SITE SITE SITE SITE SECTION
FIRST SECOND THIRD FOURTH PLAN PLAN

It will take a great deal of time and practice to develop a good lettering style. Look at others' work and strive for consistent quality and letter shapes. Lettering is different than "printing", in that you go slowly and "draw" each letter individually.   The aesthetic of the lettered page is as important as clarity and legibility. It is better not to begin with anything too fancy. Instead, copy ood examples of architectural lettering. You want to develop a style, but not look too far out.   Always use 2 or 3 guide lines for your lettering (and numbers) every time you letter on a plan. The guide lines should be lightly scribed and need not be erased.   They contribute to the accepted texture of an architectural plan and, if lightly done, won't usually show up on a blue print. I have provided a page of typical lettering styles for you to experiment with, and there are many other examples represented in plates in this book. I have also provided a typical practice sheet for you to reproduce and use for practice. The guidelines should be very light so they do not trick the eye. Always practice with your drafting pencil, as pens and other instruments give false practice.

LETTERING EXAMPLES

ABCDEFGHIJKLMNOPQRSTUV
WXYZ 0123456189
ABCDEFGHIJKLMNOPQRSTU
VWXYZ 0123456189
ABCDEFGHIJKLMNOPQRSTUVWXYZ
0123456789
ABCDEFGHIJKLMNOPQRSTUVWXYZ
0123456789

LETTERING PRACTICE SHEET

PLANS

The plan is a birds-eye view of an object. In the case of an architectural plan, the building is viewed as if it has been sliced in two horizontally, about three or four feet above the floor. This view with the roof removed shows all the window and door openings and interior walls.

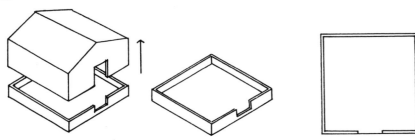

A site plan is an architectural birds-eye view with the roof on, and depicts the yard, ground, parking, etc. Interior design plans usually show furniture, rugs, and other objects resting on the floor. Other specialized plan views include: electrical and plumbing; reflected ceiling; mechanical; etc.

There are various stages in the development of an architectural plan. First is the sketch or schematic. Usually a freehand drawing, this is where the idea is hatched, an many sketches are discarded before the designer moves on to the next phase.

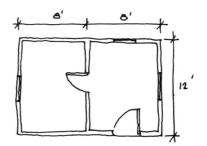

The preliminary design plan follows the sketch and is a drafted plan, but without all the details and dimensions.

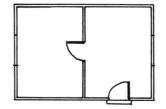

Then comes the presentation plan. This is often rendered to show texture and materials, and is often colored with pencils and/or other markers. This is for a formal client presentation to gain approval for the designer to continue into the working drawing stage.

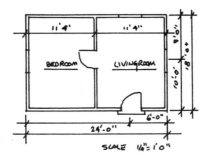

This final version of the plan gives all the information, in combination with elevations and details, such as sections, that the contractor or carpenters need to construct or install the building or interior design exactly the way the designer and the owner wish.

Often the presentation phase is left out, and sometimes this phase is as far as a design gets. All three are related in a developmental sequence from idea to actuality.

Sketch or schematic plans are best worked out to scale rather than by eye because at small scales like 1/4" or 1/8", it is very easy to be fooled by a fraction of an inch. This can be drawn quickly, however, with pencil or felt-tip pen on inexpensive roll tracing paper. The designer can then make overlay tracing after tracing, to refine and develop the design idea before drafting a more rigid and time-consuming preliminary. Quickness should be emphasized--but remember scale. Never stop with the first sketch, even though you might come back to it in the end. The more ideas you try, the better the design. In interior design plans, where the walls are fixed by others, the designer can cut paper shapes to scale to represent furniture, and move them about until the final solution is selected.

The preliminary should be drafted just as if it is going to be the final working drawing, but stopped short of all the dimensions and details. At this stage, designers often have a blueprint company make an *ozalid* "sepia" on tracing velum that can be used for the presentation plan, reserving the original tracing to be completed into working drawings.

The working plan should contain every dimension and detail that a contractor of tradesperson might ask for on the job, and it should be extremely accurate. This prevents mistakes, many phone calls to the designer, and law suits from dissatisfied clients. The drawings should be as neat, organized and uncluttered as possible, and at the same time, complete.

Dimensions should be drawn from the center of objects and walls to the center of other reference points when you want to show overall size and layout. Furniture and other objects are dimensioned from the outside edges to the outside edges. Exterior walls of buildings are also dimensioned from the outside edges. When a dimension line is drawn from an exterior wall to an interior wall, it should be from the outside of the exterior to the center of the interior wall. This method of sizing walls and objects from the center does not depend on knowing exactly the thickness of panels, plaster, etc., when the building is laid out or designed, and therefore is simpler and more accurate with fewer measurements.

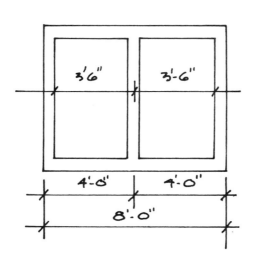
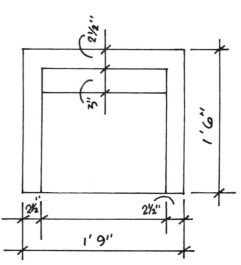

STEP BY STEP PLAN

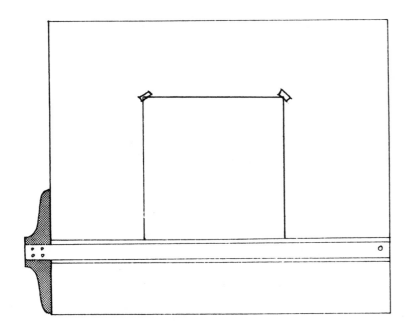

1.   Square paper and tape to board.

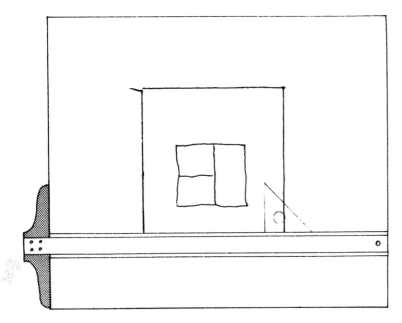

2.   Rough out general dimensions of plan so it is balanced well on the page.

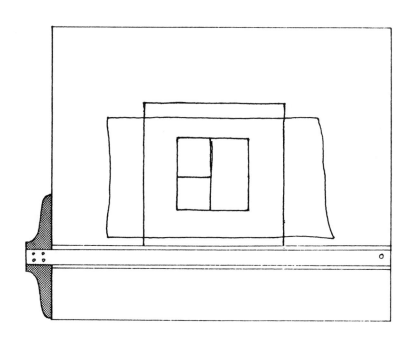

3.   Use canary or other inexpensive tracing overlay until final plan is devised.

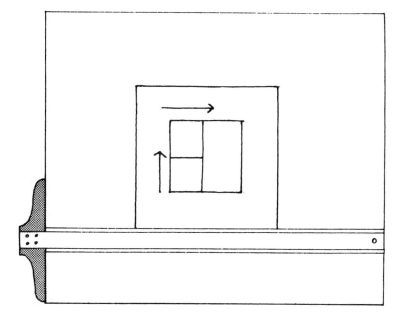

4.   (Draw lightly.) Draw all exterior dimensions of plan. Start in one corner and work systematically around plan.

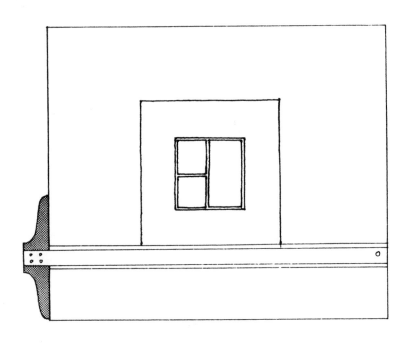

5.   (Draw lightly.) Add wall thicknesses and interior walls.   Work outside to inside in all directions.

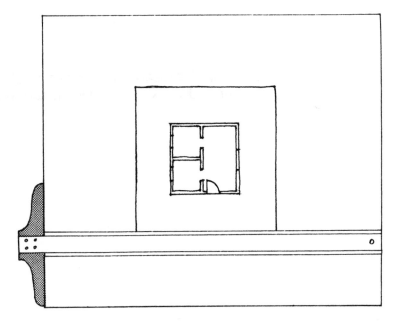

6.   (Draw lightly.) Check all door and window openings.

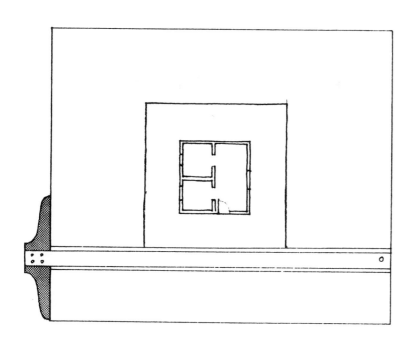

7.   (Heavy lines.) Darken and finalize lines. Erase construction lines and mistakes.

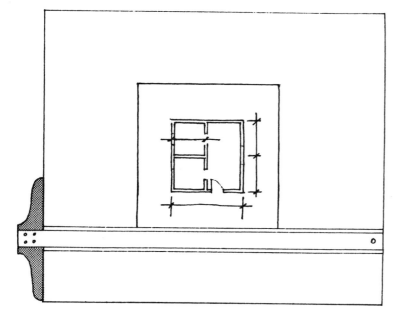

8.   Add details such as furniture, texture, dimension lines, etc.

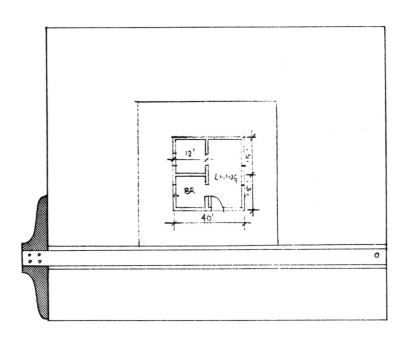

9.   Finally, letter all dimensions, notes, etc.

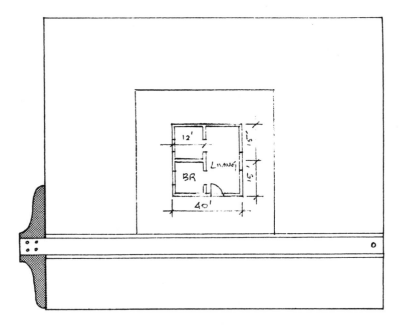

10.   Clean drawing with art gum, etc.

"AS BUILT" PLAN

Often interior designers find themselves designing and remodeling existing architectural spaces. In this case, the working plans for the building may not be available, or if available, they may not be accurate. The interior designer then must measure and draw up the plan from the existing building. The drafting technique in this case is the same as for any other plan, but the dimensions won't go to the center of the interior walls and the exterior of the exterior walls. Rather, they will be indicated from the face of existing wall to face of existing wall. Any new construction indicated on the same plan should revert to the same rules for new construction. The new construction should also be indicated as such on the "as built" plan.

"AS BUILT" OR MEASURED DRAWINGS

HOW TO START:

There are some basic tools that make measuring an existing space easier. They are: 1) a good, sturdy, legal-size yellow pad; 2) a wide, 25-foot metal tape measure; 3) a #2 pencil; 4) a six- foot wooden folding rule; 5) an assistant, if possible; and 6) a ladder, if there are tall elements to measure.

The first thing you should do before you start actually measuring is to look carefully at the entire space you are measuring and, in particular, at the individual details you will need to know about when you get back to your drawing board. Don't assume you will remember how anything looks, as there are always so many details that they eventually run together in memory.

After you have thoroughly looked and planned your approach, take your yellow pad and sketch every area you are to measure in a plan view. Include every detail you will measure. Give yourself enough room for dimensions and notes. You may need a sheet for each room and extras for windows, cabinets, and special elements such as fireplaces and stairs. You should also have an overall sketch that at least shows how everything fits together.

When you have completed your notes, it is time to start measuring. Measure the perimeter of each room, and include such details as door and window moulding widths and shapes, directions of door swings, window sizes, door and window jamb heights, odd angles, etc. Be sure to estimate wall thickness at door openings. This will help you when you piece the drawings together into a complete plan later. Note the location of any details of which you have made separate drawings, so that you can key the finished drawing at your drawing board.

When you are drafting up the results of your field trip, remember that it is best to round off measurements in large areas to the nearest 1" or 1 1/2 ", but that details such as mouldings should not be rounded off. You will discover that some areas don't seem to match up, especially when you start piecing several rooms together. This will require some discretion in compensating for the discrepancies. Some "fudging" of the dimensions will occur if you want to remain sane. Don't let it worry you, but if you find a lot of problems, it might be necessary to go back to the site with your tape measure and partially completed drafting to check the measurements again. It is also best to draft up the "as built" plans from your notes as soon as possible after measuring. The colder the notes, the more problems you will have.

Finally, any access to original architectural plans of a space will save much time in developing "as built" plans, even if there have been many changes in the space. A word of caution, however-- don't assume the original contractor followed the plans to the inch! Check even complete plans against measurements of the actual building for accuracy. You might be surprised at the minor but significant changes you find, and at the details that didn't get into the plans that might affect your interior design intentions.

OTHER THINGS TO NOTE: Electrical outlets and switches, beam locations (make dotted lines to indicate these), ceiling height changes or details, actual door widths (for replacement doors), types of materials encountered (woods, etc.), details of cabinets, etc.

A Polaroid or 35mm camera is extremely valuable for documenting as much as possible about the space for your design files.

"AS BUILT" PLAN

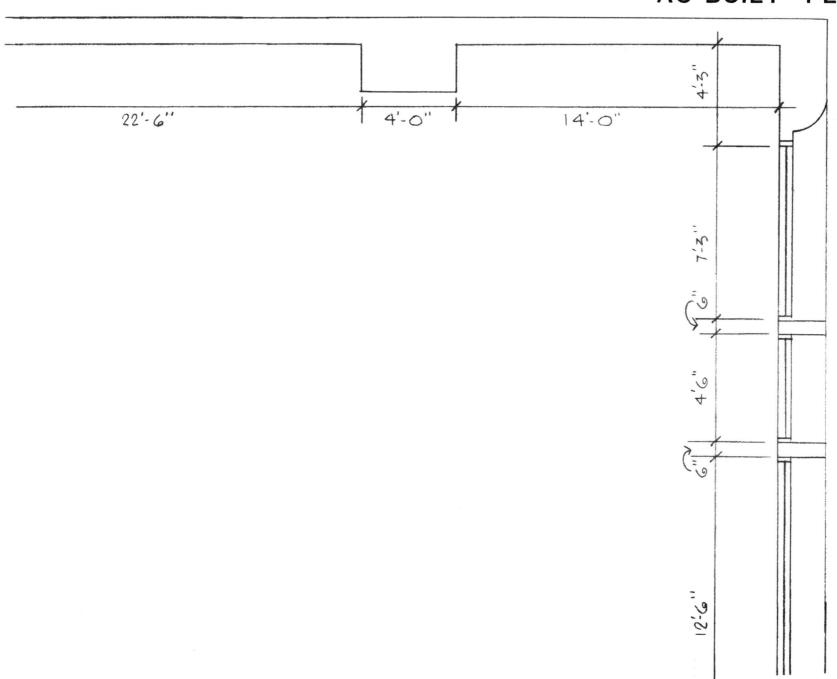

WORKING PLAN

The Working Plan or Construction Drawing represents all the basic horizontal layout information and dimensions needed by the contractors or trades-people to build the design.

The graphics in this plan must be accurate and consistent. All the dimensions should be consistent and double-checked before they are transmitted to the contractor. The line quality has a great bearing both on the communication of the design and on the image of professionalism they project.

Remember that you are drawing a tracing that will be *Diazo*-printed for distribution, and that both quality tracing paper and good, dark, clear lines are demanded.

WORKING PLAN

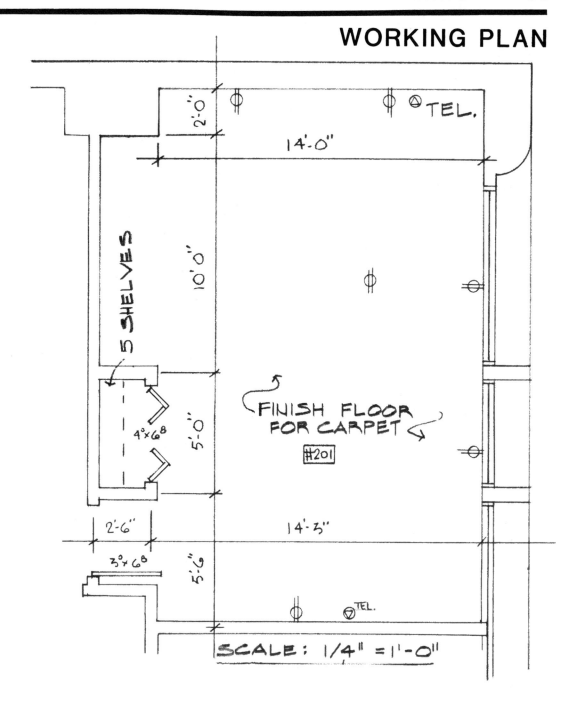

2'-0"

14'-0"

TEL.

5 SHELVES

10'-0"

FINISH FLOOR
FOR CARPET

#201

4⁰×6⁸

5'-0"

2'-6"

14'-3"

3⁰×6⁸

5'-6"

TEL.

SCALE: 1/4" = 1'-0"

PRESENTATION PLAN

The Presentation Plan is often an early layout of the walls and furniture elements in a design project to show to the client for approval of the design concept. It is important that the Presentation Plan be clear and succinct. It is usually textured and rendered with wood grain and other details to give it life and make it easy for a non-professional to read. This is one of the few times that ink drawing may be indicated in interior design drafting. Often a blue, brown or black line *Diazo* print is made of the plans and drawing, then mounted on ilustration board and colored with markers or pencils. The original is usually kept in the office, as are design tracings and tracings of working drawings.

PRESENTATION PLAN

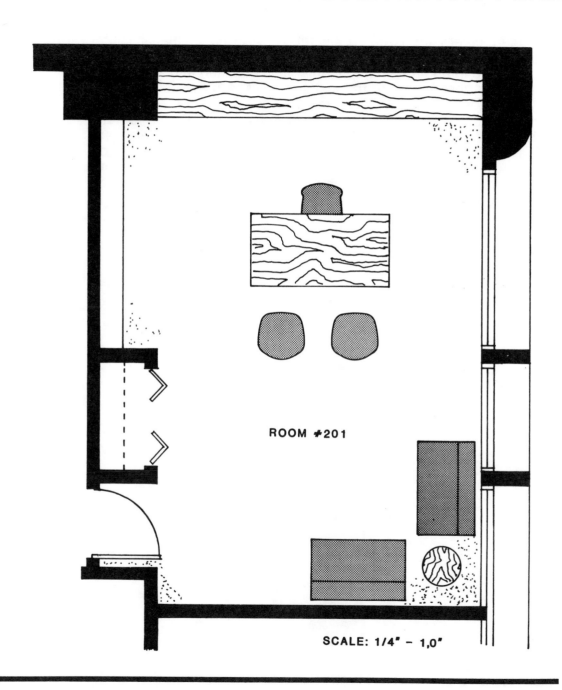

ROOM #201

SCALE: 1/4" – 1,0"

FURNITURE PLAN

This plan differs from the Presentation Drawing in that it is not usually textured, and has clear indicators of the final placement of furniture and interior design elements. It is also tied into a furniture schedule or description for the installer. These may be drawn for an entire floor, or room by room, depending on the scale and complexity of the project, or they may be drawn up in both formats in the same or different scales. 1/8", 1/4", and 1/2" scales are typical for furniture layouts. Templates are the easiest way to do the drawing, and both general and brand-name templates are available. Brand-name templates are available from many furniture manufacturers, including *Herman Miller*, *Knoll*, and *Steelcase*.

FURNITURE PLAN

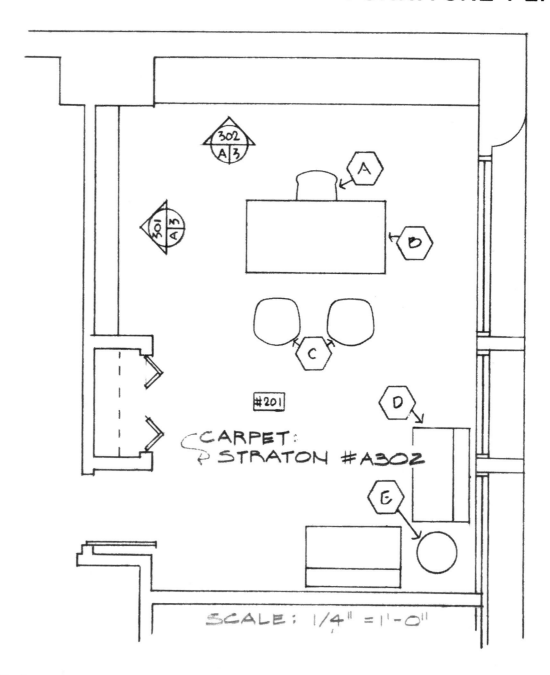

CARPET:
STRATON #A302

#201

SCALE: 1/4" = 1'-0"

REFLECTED CEILING PLAN

A Reflected Ceiling Plan is a ceiling plan drawn as if the ceiling is reflected into a mirror on the room floor, as the drafter is looking down at the image. This allows the floor and ceiling plans to line up on the drafting board, and helps coordinate all the ceiling and lighting elements with the furniture and floor elements. Sometimes the Reflected Ceiling Plan will only indicate level changes and decoration on the ceiling; sometimes only the lighting equipment; sometimes, both. Occasionally, the electrical circuitry is also indicated on the Reflected Ceiling Plan, but most often there is a separate electrical plan provided by the electrical engineer. I have included examples of several types of ceiling plans, as well as a symbol sheet for electrical and lighting equipment. Remember that scale is important, both to the eye and to the scale rule.

REFLECTED CEILING PLAN

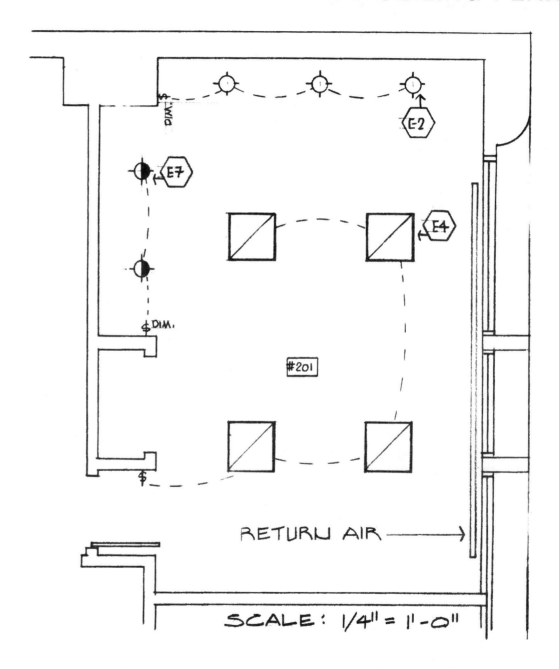

RETURN AIR ⟶

SCALE: 1/4" = 1'-0"

ELEVATIONS

Elevations are merely vertical, rather than horizontal, "plans" of a wall or building element. The same principles apply to elevation drawing, except they rarely show cut-away elements as do plans.

ELEVATION

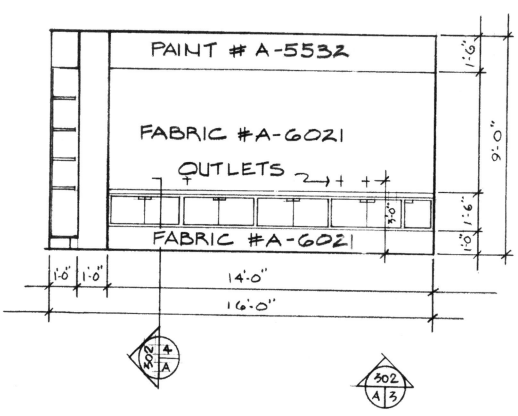

PAINT # A-5532

FABRIC #A-6021

OUTLETS

FABRIC #A-6021

1'-6"

9'-0"

1'-6"

3'-0"

1'-0"

1'-0"   1'-0"

14'-0"

16'-0"

204 4 A

302 A 3

SCALE: 1/4" = 1'-0"

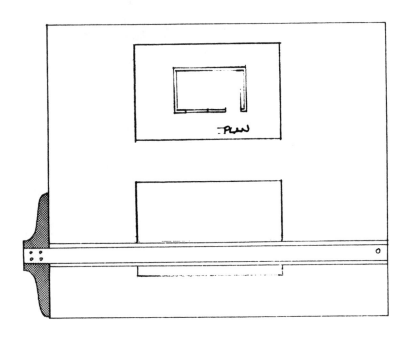

STEP BY STEP ELEVATIONS

1.   Place your plan on your board above your clean sheet, so that the side of the plan you wish to draw the elevation of is in line with your clean sheet.

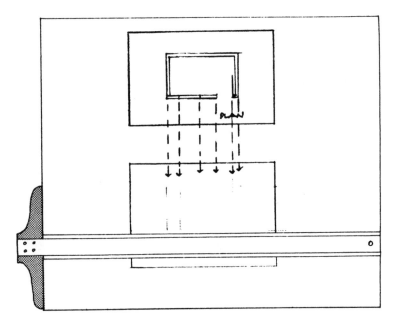

2.   Drop the measurements with your triangle from the plan to the elevation sheet.

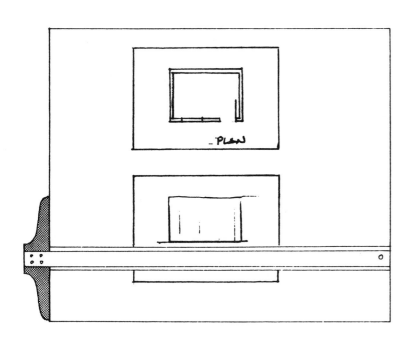

3.   Establish the base line of your elevation.

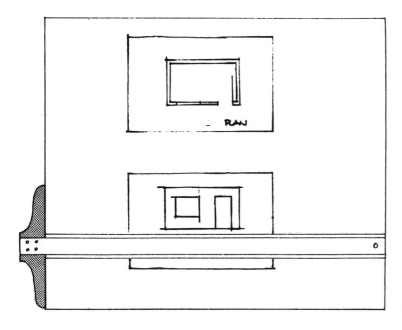

4.   Measure up from the base line along the vertical lines derived from you plan, to establish the sizes and locations of doors, windows, and other horizontal lines. These measurements can come from section drawings, if available.

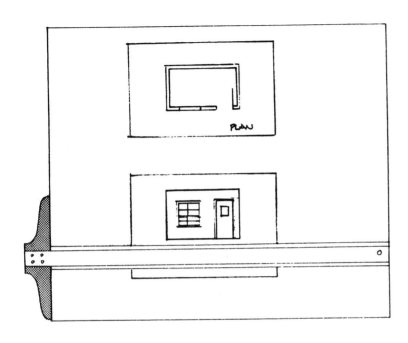

5.   Clean up your construction lines.

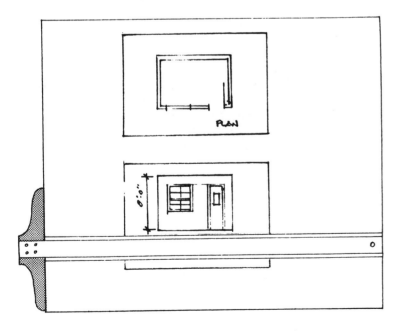

6.   Put in any dimensions and notes necessary to convey the size and construction of the object.

INTERIOR ELEVATIONS

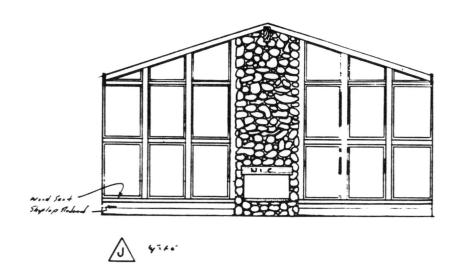

Wood Seat
Shiplap Redwood

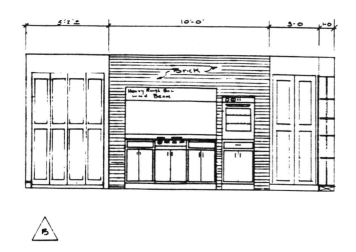

Brick

Heavy Rough Sawn Wood Beam

W.C

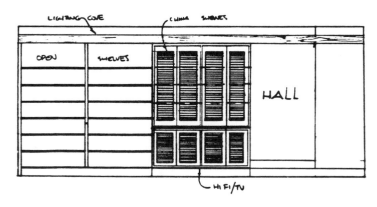

LIGHTING COVE   CHINA SHELVES

OPEN   SHELVES

HALL

HI FI/TU

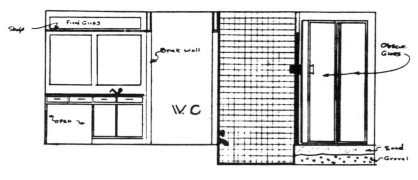

Shelf   Fixed Glass

Brick Wall

W.C

OPEN

Obscur. Glass

Sand Gravel

J

B

G

E

SECTIONS

Sections are usually vertical cutaway views that show in two dimensions the construction elements of an area of the building, furniture or construction. They use the same principles as plan and elevation, but they are usually drawn at a larger scale. Often elevations and sections are combined in the same drawing for cabinets and interior elements.

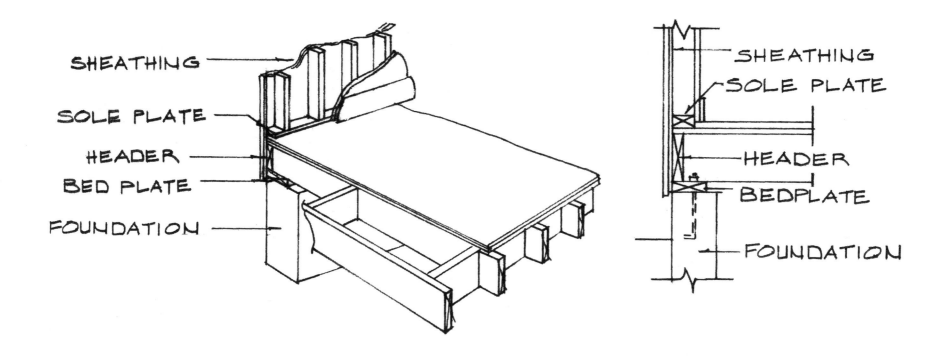

SHEATHING

SOLE PLATE

HEADER

BED PLATE

FOUNDATION

SHEATHING

SOLE PLATE

HEADER

BEDPLATE

FOUNDATION

CABINET SECTION

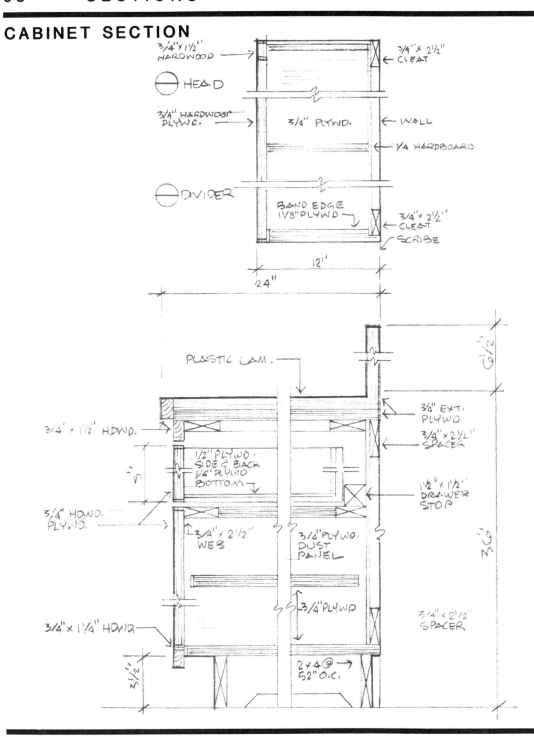

3/4" x 1 1/2" HARDWOOD

3/4" x 2 1/2" CLEAT

HEAD

3/4" HARDWOOD PLYWD.

3/4" PLYWD.

WALL

1/4 HARDBOARD

DIVIDER

BAND EDGE 1 1/8" PLYWD

3/4" x 2 1/2" CLEAT

SCRIBE

12"

24"

PLASTIC LAM.

3/4" EXT. PLYWD

3/4" x 2 1/2" SPACER

3/4" x 1 1/2" HDWD.

1/2" PLYWD. SIDE & BACK 1/4" PLYWD BOTTOM

1 1/2" x 1 1/2" DRAWER STOP

3/4" HDWD. PLYWD.

3/4" x 2 1/2" WEB

3/4" PLYWD. DUST PANEL

3/4" PLYWD

3/4" x 2 1/2" SPACER

36"

6 1/2"

3/4" x 1 1/4" HDWD.

2 1/2"

2 x 4 @ 52" O.C.

DETAILS

A detail is a drawing that describes exactly how a particular element of a design goes together. It also describes the material from which it is made. The plans and elevations give the general information, while the detail gives the specifics. For example, the general location of cabinets would be given on the plan and on the elevation, while the detail would show the actual thickness of the wood fascia, and the shape and size of the door edges and hardware.

Plans are usually drawn at 1/8", 1/4" or 1/2" scale, or in some cases even in full scale. This "magnification" allows maximum information to show. The larger the scale, the more precise the detail will be. You must judge the amount of information required by the carpenter or cabinet maker and respond accordingly.

While it is true that a great deal of information is required to make sure that your ideas are being followed by the cabinet maker or craftsperson, it is often the case that specific machines and materials are unique to a particular craftsperson or shop, and it is difficult to anticipate all these variables in the design stage. It is important that the designer communicate with the craftsperson to find out his or her capabilities and requirements, and how these might affect the design. This might be done as the original drawing is prepared, or the designer might require the craftsperson to submit "shop drawings" to show the final and detailed constructions that will be utilized in the project.

Because of the interface with the craftsperson over the "shop drawing", it is not necessary for the Design Details to call out every nail and screw. You need to indicate only those important details and the elements you do not wish to leave up to the choice of the craftsperson. In other words, plans are the least specific, detail are the next, and shop drawings are the most specific.

RULES OF DETAILING

1. Be specific and accurate. Draw the object as it is built, in that sequence. Think through every place where the craftsperson might go wrong.

2. Be logical in your graphic arrangement.

3. Make all the notes and views clear and label them neatly.

4. In notes, sizes usually come first, then the name of the piece, spacing, and finally, any other information.

5. The inside of a building or element is always drawn from right to left, the outside is drawn from left to right.

6. Always use the actual size of wood and other materials in detail drawings. When you draw a 2x4 (a 2x4 actually measures 1 1/2 x 3 1/2), remember that lumber is noted as it is named (nominal size, i.e., 2x4), even though it is drawn its actual size. Milled or special materials such as moulding or plywood are drawn and noted in their actual sizes.

7.   Notes and leaders should never interfere with, but should rather enhance, the neatness and clarity of the drawings.

8.   Each detail should stand alone with its own notes, as much as possible.

9.   Brand name materials and items should be avoided in a "bid" project, though they are perfectly appropriate in a job where they are agreed upon with the client.

10.   Abbreviations and slang should be avoided in notes, except in trade standard usages. Check the Architectural Graphic Standards or other sources for such abbreviations.

11.   Dimension Types:

    (a)   A dimension written simply will be held by the craftsperson within reasonable tolerances.

    (b)   A dimension with "minimum" next to it may be larger, but not smaller.

    (c)   A dimension with "maximum" next to it may be smaller, but not larger.

    (d)   "Not to Scale" should be noted if that is the case of the drawing.

    (e)   "Hold" means that the dimension is highly critical and must be maintained at all cost.

    (f)   "Varies" means that the dimension may fluctuate.

12.   Fractions should be avoided when possible, and should conform to 1/8" or 1/4" increments, if used.

13.   Materials should be clearly indicated in symbol form.

14.   Profile drawings show that the shape and outline stand out. They also give a "3-D" effect, and allow the drawing to be read more easily.

15.   Reference notes and keys to the plans and elevations should always be used so that the craftsperson can see where the detail drawing occurs in the overall scheme.

SUGGESTED MINIMUM REQUIREMENTS FOR ARCHITECTURAL DRAWINGS OF CASEWORK AND PLASTIC TOPS

Elevations for conventional casework should be shown on the architectural drawings as suggested below.

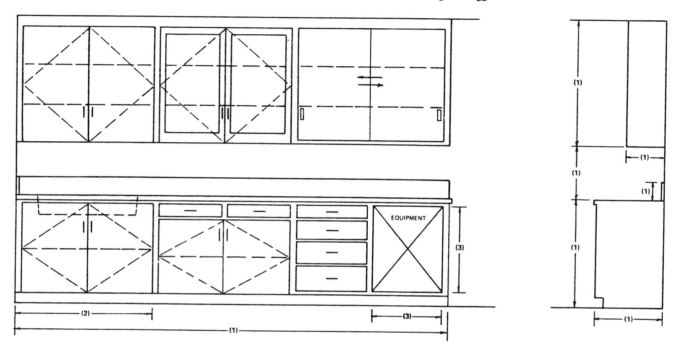

The following information should be included on the floor plan or elevations for casework:

(1) Indicate basic overall dimensions.
(2) Indicate dimensions of those portions which are required to be of predetermined or controlled size.
(3) Indicate dimensions required for installation of items of equipment.
(4) Indicate whether face frame construction or flush overlay type construction.
(5) Indicate whether lipped or flush installation of doors and drawers if face frame construction.
(6) Indicate whether sliding or hinged doors, including swing if hinged.
(7) Indicate thickness of cabinet doors if other than 3/4" is required.
(8) The only details required to be shown are those not shown in the W.I.C. Manual or those which involve installation of unusual equipment in the casework.
(9) Note if and where locks are required.
(10) Indicate shelves and note whether fixed or adjustable. Do not indicate thickness of shelves unless modification of W.I.C. standards is desired.
(11) Indicate kind of top. See Sections 16 and 17 for plan requirements.

VANITY BASE STANDARDS

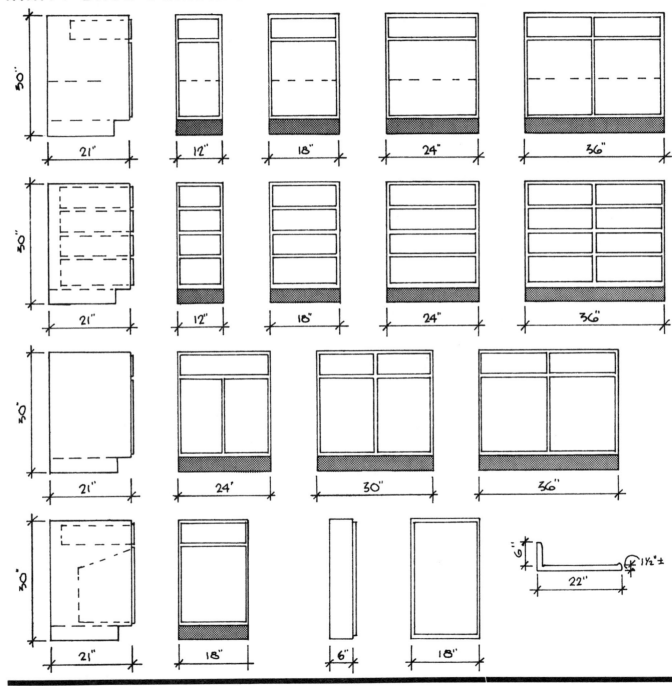

BASE CABINET STANDARDS

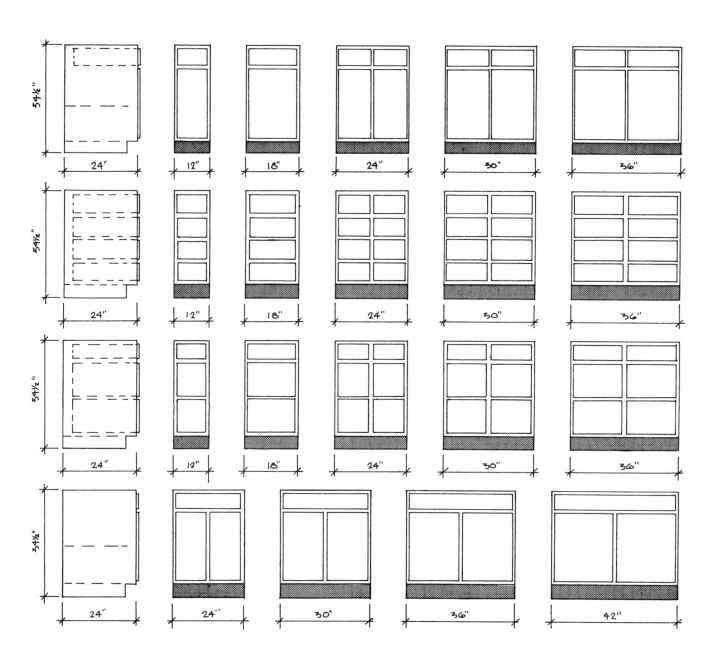

OVERHEAD CABINET STANDARDS

SUGGESTED MINIMUM SIZES FOR PARTS OF A CABINET

Face frame	3/4"
Ends and divisions	
Flush overlay	3/4"
Economy	1/2"
Custom premium	5/8"
Shelves	
Economy	
Solid stock or	
particleboard	3/4"
Plywood	5/8"
Custom and premium	3/4"
Length	
Over 3'-6" in length and adjustable	1"
Over 4'-0" in length and adjustable	1"
Tops and bottoms	
Economy	Same as shelves
Custom and premium	3/4"
Length over 4-'0"	1"
Web members or stretcher	3/4" x 2"
Backs	
Economy untempered hardboard	1/8"
Custom and premium--Plywood	
or tempered hardboard	1/4"
Exposed backs	3/4"
Breadboards	3/4"
Drawers	
Side, sub fronts, and backs	
Economy	7/16"
Custom and premium	1/2"
Bottoms	
Economy (18" maximum	1/8"
width)	
Economy (over 18")	1/4"
Custom and premium	1/4"
Cabinet door faces	
All grades	3/4"

Construction methods, lumber and material sizes, and dimensions of furniture and cabinets are all extremely important in developing an interior design plan.   No designer can remember all this information, therefore it is important to become familiar with references and begin to collect a library of them.

Nominal Rough	Douglas Fir Hemlock Western Red Cedar		Redwood		Ponderosa Pine Sugar Pine	
	Thickness	Width	Thickness	Width	Thickness	Width
1"	$\frac{11}{16}$"		$\frac{11}{16}$"		$\frac{3}{4}$"	
$1\frac{1}{4}$"	$\frac{15}{16}$"		1"		1"	
$1\frac{1}{2}$"	$1\frac{3}{16}$"				$1\frac{1}{4}$"	
2"	$1\frac{7}{16}$"	$1\frac{1}{2}$"	$1\frac{1}{2}$"	$1\frac{1}{2}$"	$1\frac{1}{2}$"	$1\frac{1}{2}$"
3"	$2\frac{7}{16}$"	$2\frac{1}{2}$"	$2\frac{1}{2}$"	$2\frac{1}{2}$"	$2\frac{1}{2}$"	$2\frac{1}{2}$"
4"	$3\frac{7}{16}$"	$3\frac{1}{4}$"	$3\frac{1}{2}$"	$3\frac{1}{2}$"	$3\frac{1}{2}$"	$3\frac{1}{2}$"
5"		$4\frac{1}{4}$"		$4\frac{1}{2}$"		$4\frac{1}{2}$"
6"		$5\frac{1}{4}$"		$5\frac{1}{2}$"		$5\frac{1}{2}$"
8"		7"		$7\frac{1}{4}$"		$7\frac{1}{4}$"
10"		9"		$9\frac{1}{4}$"		$9\frac{1}{4}$"
12"		11"		$11\frac{1}{4}$"		$11\frac{1}{4}$"
Over 12"		1" Off		$\frac{3}{4}$" Off		$\frac{3}{4}$" Off

VENEER CORE

All plies are veneer — less than ¼" thick. Middle ply is called the "center." Plies on either side of the center, but beneath the outer plies, are called "crossbandings." Outer plies are called "faces" and "backs." Thickness varies from 1/8" to ¾" or more — odd number of plies from 3 to 11 or more.

LUMBER CORE

Center ply, called the "core" is composed of strips of lumber edge-glued into a solid slab. This type is usually 5-ply, ¾" thick but other thicknesses from ½" to 1-1/8" are manufactured for special uses. There are three main core types:

a. **Staved** — all strips random length, butt-joined.

b. **Full-Length** — all strips one-piece.

c. **Banded** — outside strips full-length, others random length. Banding may be same type of lumber as rest of core but is usually a different species. Banding may include all four edges. Banded plywood is almost always produced for special uses — furniture, desk tops, and cupboard doors.

PARTICLEBOARD CORE

Medium density boards made from wood particles and called variously "chip board" "particleboard" or "shavings board" are being used more and more to replace lumber core in plywood. Developed from a need to increase the utilization of our remaining timber reserves, these boards stand on their own merits against solid lumber in all products where they are used interchangeably.

HARDWOOD PLYWOOD — GENERAL INFORMATION

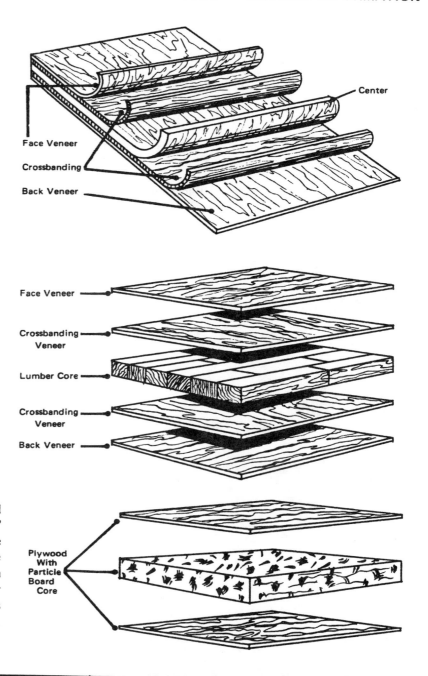

Center

Face Veneer
Crossbanding
Back Veneer

Face Veneer
Crossbanding Veneer
Lumber Core
Crossbanding Veneer
Back Veneer

Plywood With Particle Board Core

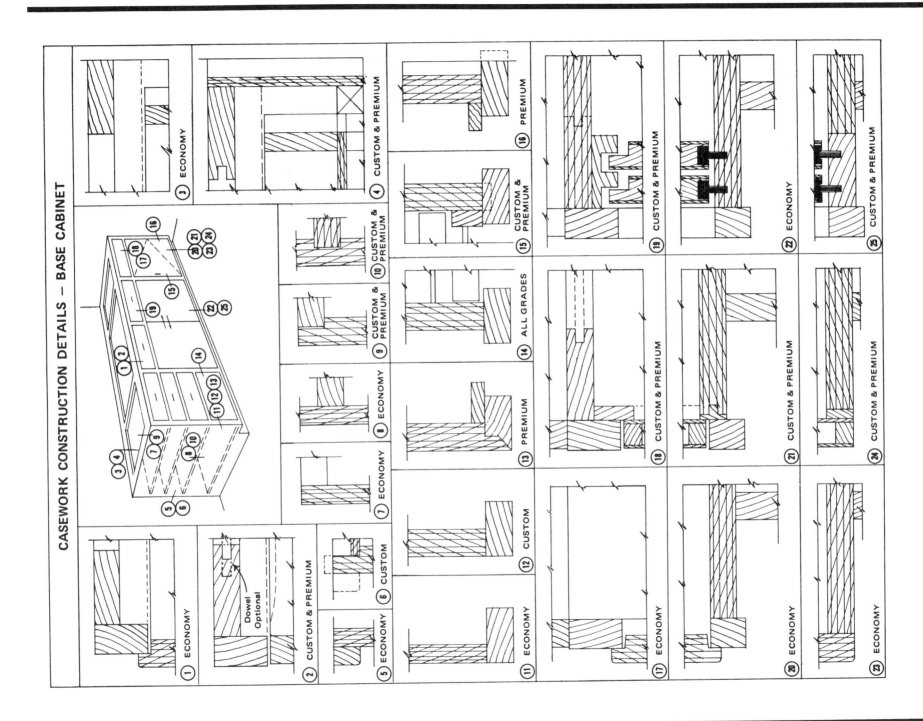

CASEWORK CONSTRUCTION DETAILS — BASE CABINET

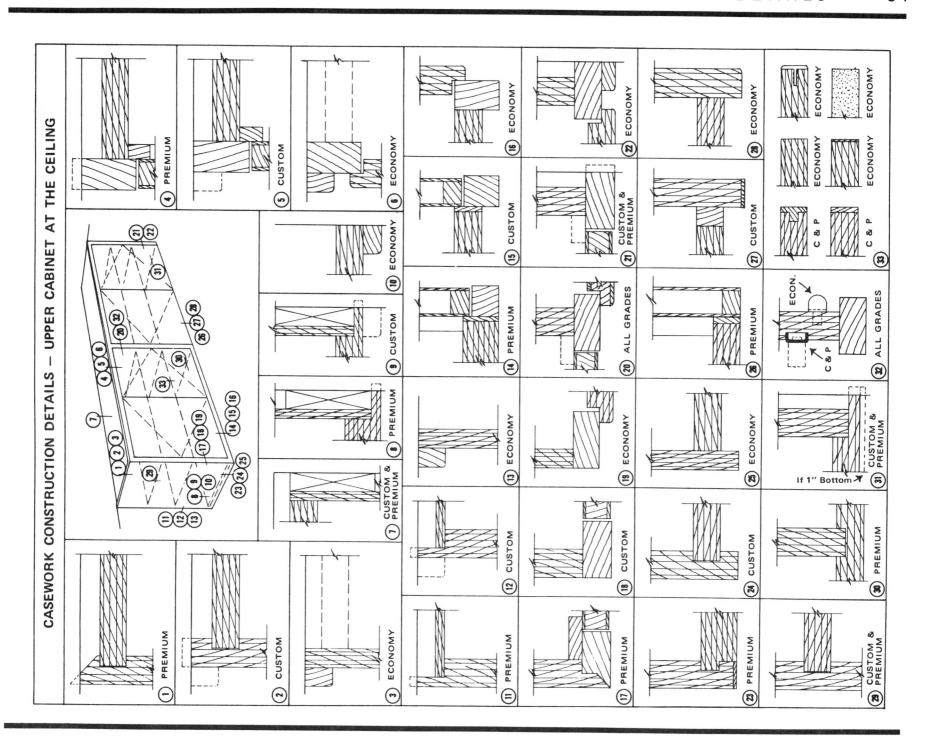

CASEWORK CONSTRUCTION DETAILS — UPPER CABINET AT THE CEILING

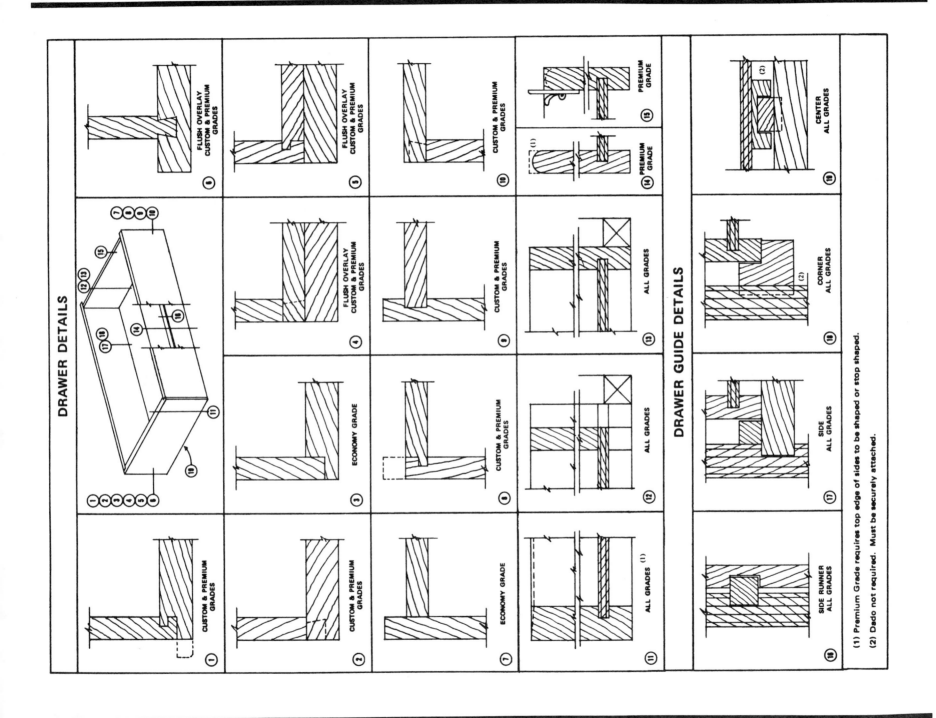

DRAWER DETAILS

DRAWER GUIDE DETAILS

(1) Premium Grade requires top edge of sides to be shaped or stop shaped.

(2) Dado not required. Must be securely attached.

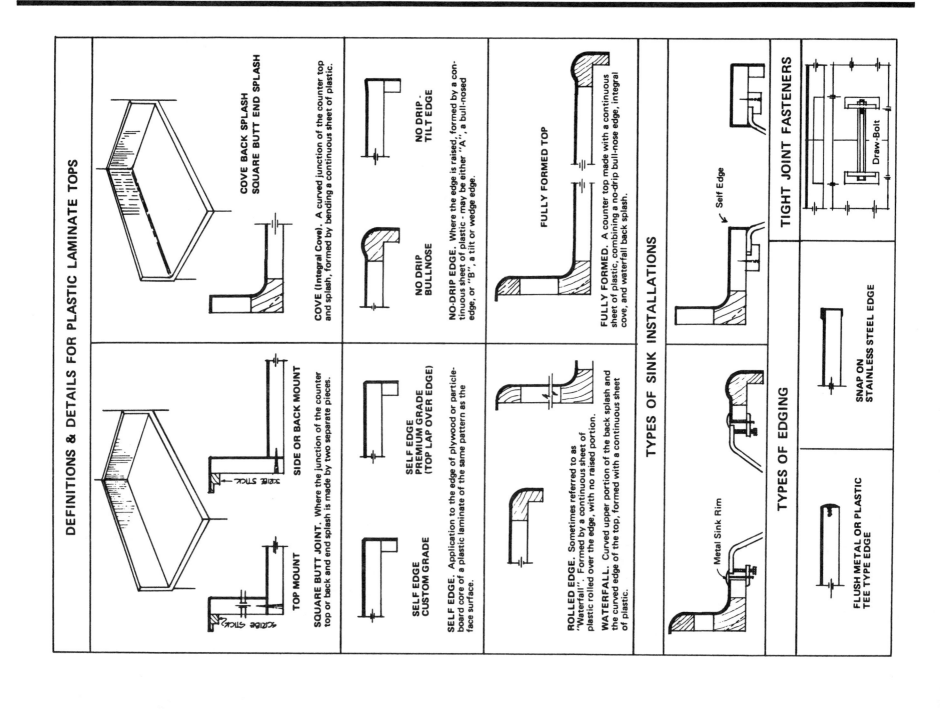

DEFINITIONS & DETAILS FOR PLASTIC LAMINATE TOPS

COVE BACK SPLASH
SQUARE BUTT END SPLASH

COVE (Integral Cove). A curved junction of the counter top and splash, formed by bending a continuous sheet of plastic.

SIDE OR BACK MOUNT

TOP MOUNT

SCRIBE STICK

SCRIBE STICK

SQUARE BUTT JOINT. Where the junction of the counter top or back and end splash is made by two separate pieces.

NO DRIP - TILT EDGE

NO DRIP BULLNOSE

NO-DRIP EDGE. Where the edge is raised, formed by a continuous sheet of plastic - may be either "A", a bull-nosed edge, or "B", a tilt or wedge edge.

SELF EDGE PREMIUM GRADE (TOP LAP OVER EDGE)

SELF EDGE CUSTOM GRADE

SELF EDGE. Application to the edge of plywood or particleboard core of a plastic laminate of the same pattern as the face surface.

FULLY FORMED TOP

FULLY FORMED. A counter top made with a continuous sheet of plastic, combining a no-drip bull-nose edge, integral cove, and waterfall back splash.

ROLLED EDGE. Sometimes referred to as "Waterfall". Formed by a continuous sheet of plastic rolled over the edge, with no raised portion.

WATERFALL. Curved upper portion of the back splash and the curved edge of the top, formed with a continuous sheet of plastic.

TYPES OF SINK INSTALLATIONS

← Self Edge

Metal Sink Rim

TIGHT JOINT FASTENERS

Draw-Bolt

TYPES OF EDGING

SNAP ON STAINLESS STEEL EDGE

FLUSH METAL OR PLASTIC TEE TYPE EDGE

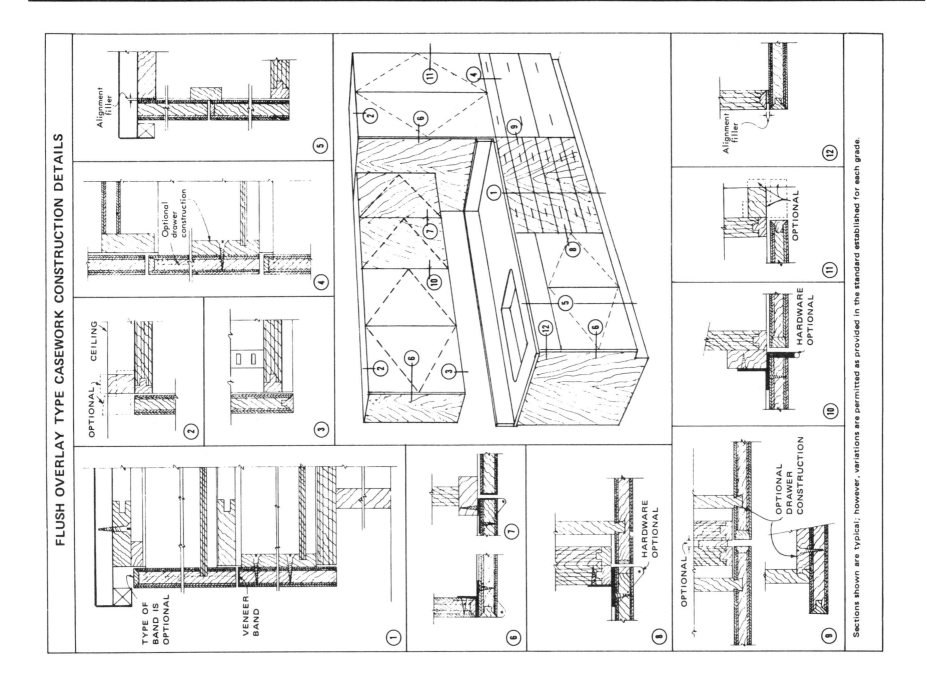

FLUSH OVERLAY TYPE CASEWORK CONSTRUCTION DETAILS

Alignment filler

Optional drawer construction

OPTIONAL   CEILING

TYPE OF BAND IS OPTIONAL

VENEER BAND

HARDWARE OPTIONAL

OPTIONAL

OPTIONAL DRAWER CONSTRUCTION

Alignment filler

HARDWARE OPTIONAL

Sections shown are typical; however, variations are permitted as provided in the standard established for each grade.

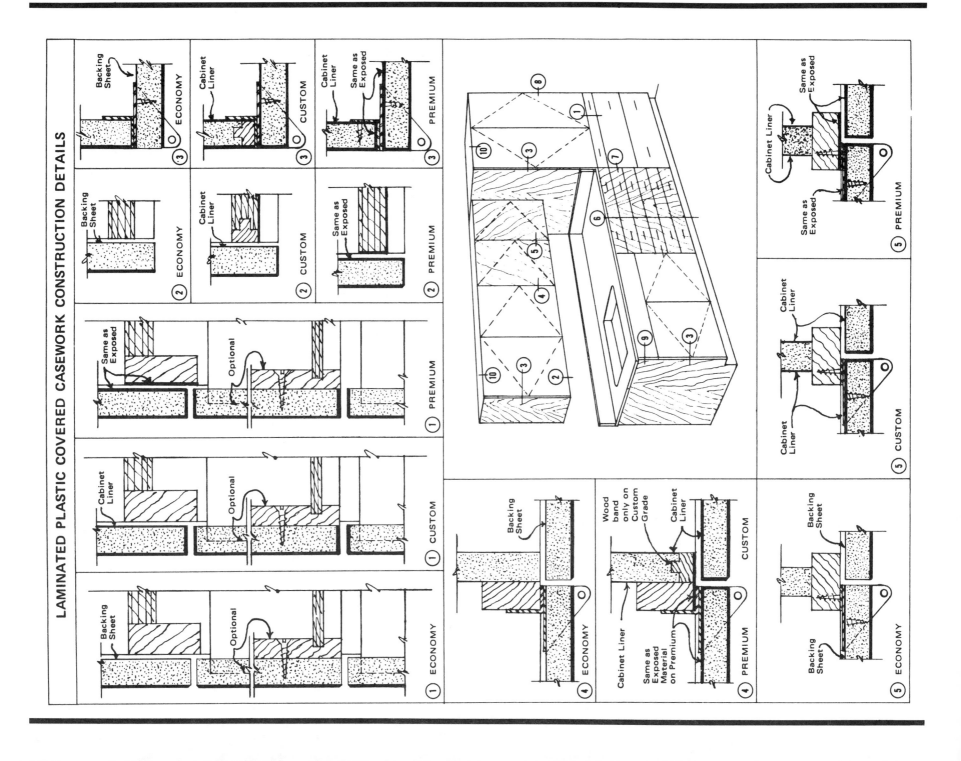

LAMINATED PLASTIC COVERED CASEWORK CONSTRUCTION DETAILS

Backing Sheet — ECONOMY ③
Cabinet Liner — CUSTOM ③
Cabinet Liner / Same as Exposed — PREMIUM ③

Backing Sheet — ECONOMY ②
Cabinet Liner — CUSTOM ②
Same as Exposed — PREMIUM ②

Same as Exposed / Optional — PREMIUM ①
Cabinet Liner / Optional — CUSTOM ①
Backing Sheet / Optional — ECONOMY ①

Backing Sheet — ECONOMY ④
Wood band only on Custom Grade / Cabinet Liner / Same as Exposed Material on Premium — PREMIUM ④
Backing Sheet — ECONOMY ⑤

Cabinet Liner / Same as Exposed — PREMIUM ⑤
Cabinet Liner / Cabinet Liner / Cabinet Liner — CUSTOM ⑤

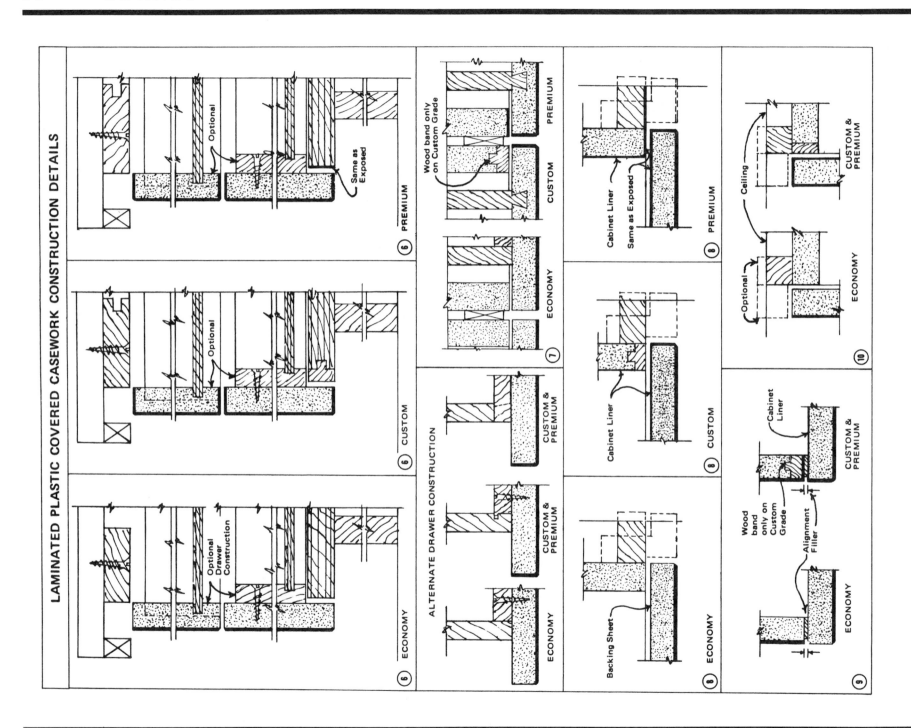

LAMINATED PLASTIC COVERED CASEWORK CONSTRUCTION DETAILS

Optional — PREMIUM — 6

Optional — CUSTOM — 6

Optional Drawer Construction — ECONOMY — 6

Wood band only on Custom Grade — PREMIUM / CUSTOM — 7

ECONOMY — 7

ALTERNATE DRAWER CONSTRUCTION — CUSTOM & PREMIUM / CUSTOM & PREMIUM / ECONOMY

Same as Exposed — Cabinet Liner — PREMIUM — 8

Cabinet Liner — CUSTOM — 8

Backing Sheet — ECONOMY — 8

Ceiling / Optional — CUSTOM & PREMIUM / ECONOMY — 10

Wood band only on Custom Grade / Cabinet Liner / Alignment Filler — CUSTOM & PREMIUM / ECONOMY — 9

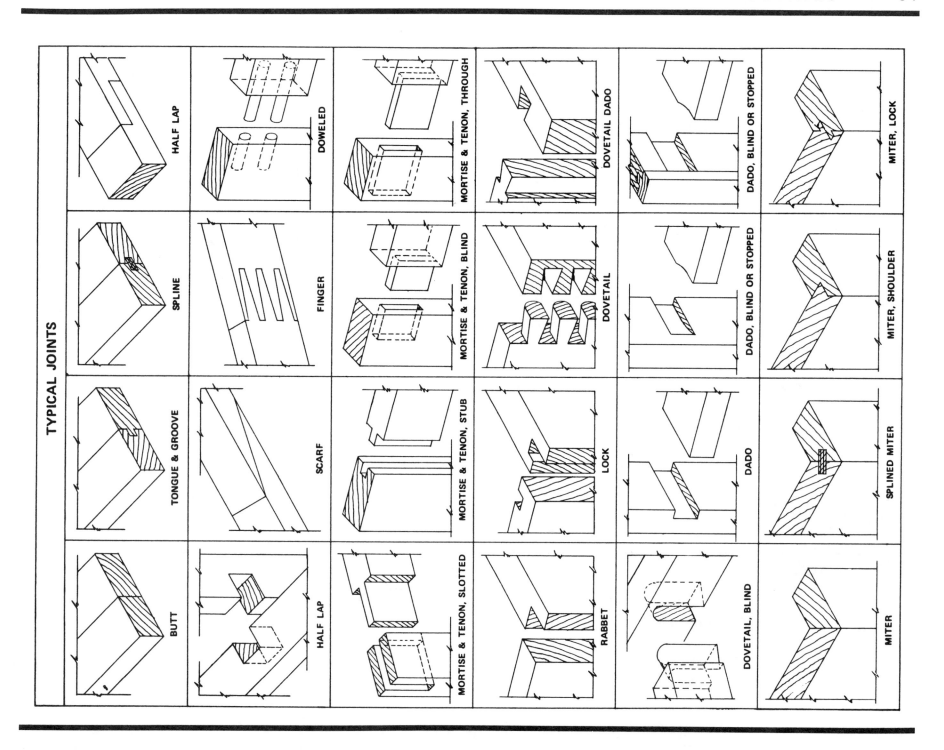

TYPICAL JOINTS

HALF LAP

DOWELED

MORTISE & TENON, THROUGH

DOVETAIL DADO

DADO, BLIND OR STOPPED

MITER, LOCK

SPLINE

FINGER

MORTISE & TENON, BLIND

DOVETAIL

DADO, BLIND OR STOPPED

MITER, SHOULDER

TONGUE & GROOVE

SCARF

MORTISE & TENON, STUB

LOCK

DADO

SPLINED MITER

BUTT

HALF LAP

MORTISE & TENON, SLOTTED

RABBET

DOVETAIL, BLIND

MITER

PROFILES OF STOCK STICKING FOR SASH AND DOORS

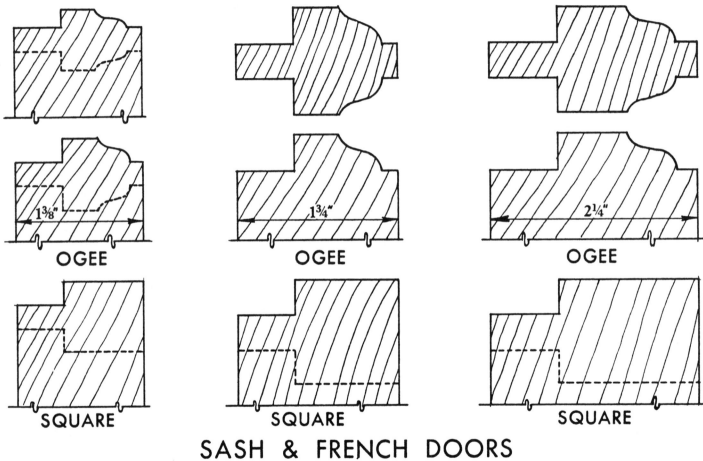

OGEE   1⅜"

OGEE   1¾"

OGEE   2¼"

SQUARE   SQUARE   SQUARE

SASH & FRENCH DOORS

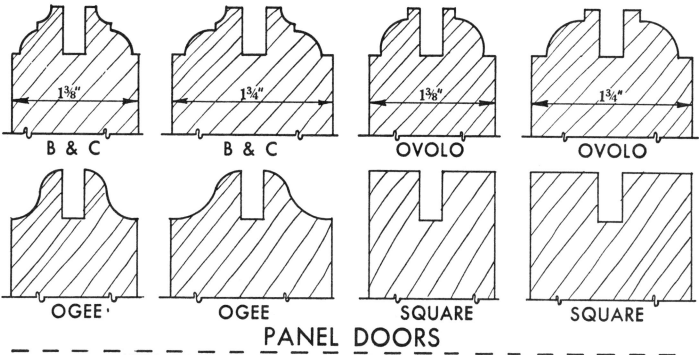

PANEL DOORS

WHEN STOCK SASH OR DOORS ARE SPECIFIED OR INDICATED THE STICKING WILL BE OPTIONAL WITH THE SUPPLIER.
SPECIAL STICKINGS FOR EITHER SASH OR DOORS INVOLVE SEVERAL SPECIAL MANUFACTURING OPERATIONS, AND ARE RELATIVELY COSTLY.

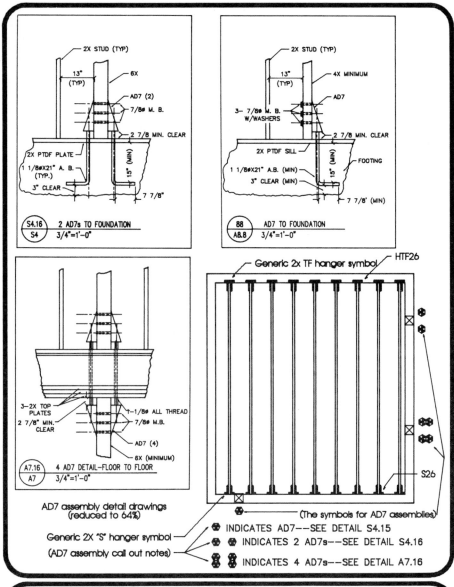

AD7 assembly detail drawings
(reduced to 64%)

Generic 2X "S" hanger symbol
(AD7 assembly call out notes)

(The symbols for AD7 assemblies)

INDICATES AD7——SEE DETAIL S4.15

INDICATES 2 AD7s——SEE DETAIL S4.16

INDICATES 4 AD7s——SEE DETAIL A7.16

SAMPLE SYMBOLS
STRUCTURAL HARDWARE
1/4" to 1'—0"   COPYRIGHT 1986 LLOYD MARTIN

CTi
Creative Technologies Inc.
4567 Branciforte Drive
Santa Cruz CA 95065
(408)426—6806

PERCEPTION

In surveying the literature of perception I encountered the classic book by James J. Gibson, *The Perception of the Visual World*, (Boston: Houghton Mifflin, 1950). This book, aside from its important place in the psychology of perception, was an exciting discovery for me because of its implication for the understanding and teaching of perspective and drawing to artists and designers.

Of Gibson's thirteen varieties of perspective "sensory shifts," I have incorporated nine into a portion of the college class I teach on perspective. I have prepared an outline of the nine concerns and line drawings to illustrate each concept from the point of view of the designer and artist.

The nine principles that I have selected are directly related to the perspectives used both intentionally and accidentally by the draftsman. The other four principles of Gibson's are related to perception of perspective in motion, or are related to binoculor vision, which is not replicated in the two-dimensional representation used in drawing.

According to Gibson, there is no such thing as perception of space without a continuous background surface. He also claims that memory and past stimulation are essential to, and the foundation of, perception in the present. His "sensory shifts", visual impressions that go with the perception of depth over a continous surface, are analogous to vowels and consonants in speech, that is, large classes of contrasting sounds. They are the basic vocabulary of visual experiences.

Gibson has analyzed and constructed the system and the "component variables" which provide the necessary information to perceive and process three dimensional visual material.   Gibson has approahed the problem as a system versus the earlier isolated thesis of perception.

Berkeley, an early theorist of perception, suggests that we use two elements to determine the size and distance of an object: the size of the image projected on the retina from the object; and previous motor sensations associated with corresponding retinal objects. According to this empirical theory of vision, our understanding of the distance and size of an object is determined by the size of the image on the retina. This is a very unlikely explanation and has very little application in drawing and projective perspectve theory.

As stated above, Gibson takes an entirely different and more wholistic view of the process. He begins with gradients and cues:

> Gradient of size and density, being in correspondence with physical distance, are stimulus correlates for a continuum of seen distance. The gradient theory accounts for the distance of all objects in the array, rather than the single object on which attention is fixed...the retinal image is evidently richer in opportunities for depth-perception than the classical theorists realized (Gibson, 1950).

As I mentioned, an exciting aspect of Gibson's system is its direct application to drawing and the teaching of perspective. Some of the perspective concepts are very difficult to understand when presented in a theoretical and mechanical way. It is much more clear to the student if perspective concepts can be related to the way we actually perceive perspective "live." It is also easier to construct perspective drawings when we understand the actual perspective vocabulary used by the human perceptual system. It is analagous to the difference between accidentally banging on a piano and discovering the E Minor Scale, versus learning the scales and then applying them to musical composition. The results will undoubtedly be more satisfactory.

The nine concepts are as follows:

1.   TEXTURE PERSPECTIVE

Texture perspective occurs when the density of the texture of a surface increases as it recedes into the distance.

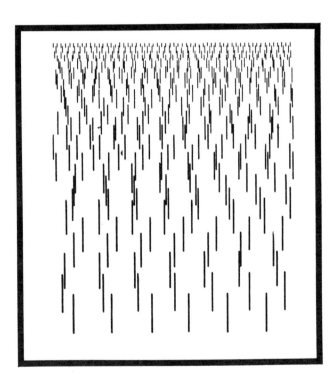

PLATE 1: TEXTURE PERSPECTIVE

2.   SIZE PERSPECTIVE

As objects recede they get smaller.

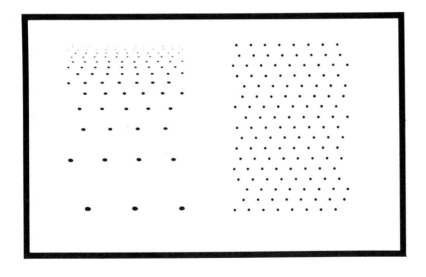

PLATE 2: SIZE PERSPECTIVE

3.   LINEAR PERSPECTIVE

In artistic terms this is one-point perspective.   Parallel lines always join at a single vanishing point at the horizon and create this illusion.

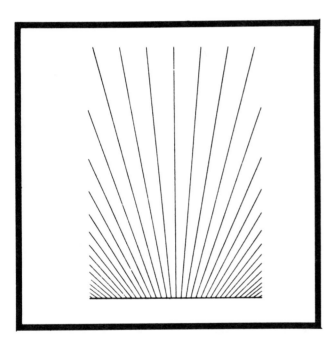

PLATE 3: LINEAR PERSPECTIVE

4.   ATMOSPHERIC PERSPECTIVE

In design terms this is a three-point perspective of infinity. It is observed in life as we observe desert mountains clearly in the distance through clear air with little haze. The illusion is that the distant object is nearby when in fact it might be fifty miles away.

PLATE 4: ATMOSPHERIC PERSPECTIVE

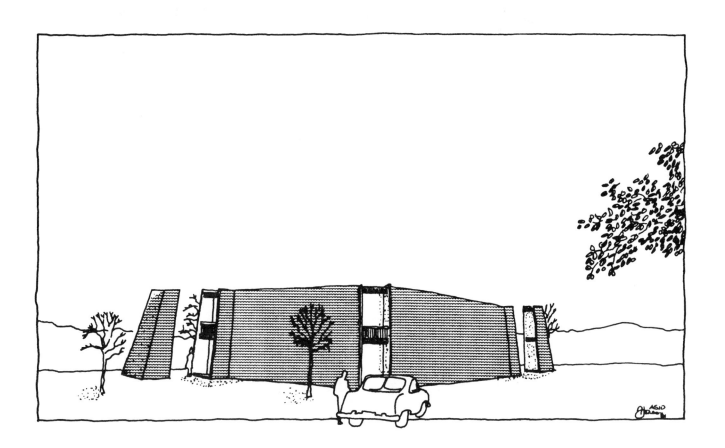

5.   THE PERSPECTIVE OF BLUR

When the eye or a camera focuses on a particular object in the foreground, the background becomes blurred, and vice versa. The artist uses this fact both overtly, and by simplifying or vignetting a drawing to create the same illusion of vision. It is much more difficult to achieve in line drawing and must be addressed indirectly by simplification of unimportant objects and domination of the lines of the "in focus" object.

PLATE 5: THE PERSPECTIVE OF BLUR

6.   RELATIVE UPWARD LOCATION IN THE VISUAL FIELD

When the horizon is eliminated from the drawing, we must rely on size gradient to gain a perspective view.

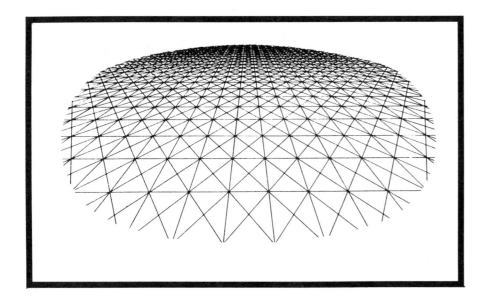

PLATE 6:   RELATIVE UPWARD LOCATION IN THE VISUAL FIELD

7.   SHIFT OF TEXTURE OF LINEAR SPACING

As Hall points out in his discussion of Gibson (Hall, 1950), this effect occurs at the edge of a cliff when you can see both immediate and distant objects sharply in the same field of vision, yet clearly in perspective.

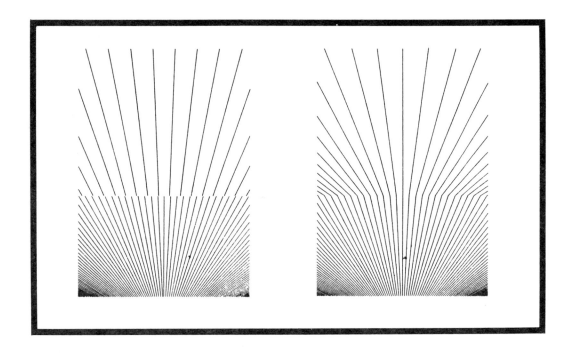

PLATE 7: SHIFT OF TEXTURE OR LINEAR SPACING

8.   COMPLETION OF CONTINUITY OF OUTLINE

When the outline of a new object is complete, and the distant one is broken, the sense of perspective is communicated. This concept has been exploited by the military in its camouflage of equipment.

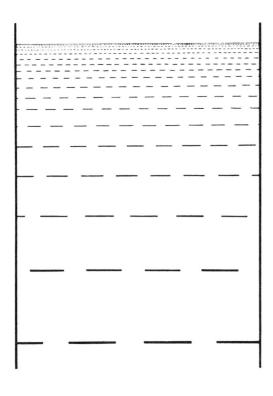

PLATE 8: COMPLETION OR CONTINUITY OF OUTLINE

9.   TRANSITION BETWEEN LIGHT AND SHADE

An abrubt change of brightness will be interpreted as the edge of an object or cliff. This is similar to the principal way we draw and see moulding or shape of objects.

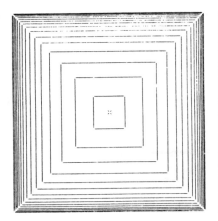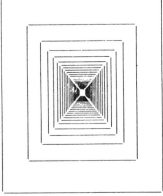

PLATE 9: TRANSITION BETWEEN LIGHT AND SHADE

The abstract plates presented here are from *The Perception of the Visual World*, (Gibson, 1950).

PERSPECTIVE

Perspective is the use of geometric shapes, angles, and lines to create the *illusion* of three-dimensional shape in a two-dimensional drawing. Perspective is a visual *language* which can be learned and used to develop and communicate ideas and designs of space and form. In particular, it is the *lingua franca* of interior design and architecture. As was demonstrated in the section on perception, the language has nouns and verbs, as well as a particular syntax.

As an interior design skill, the ability of a designer to draw and think spatially is almost primary. In spite of this fact, the skill is seldom taught and undervalued in many design programs. One of the first skills in thinking spatially should be disecting and translating the ideas to paper in the form of drawings, in much the same way language students learn to write and diagram sentences and learn grammar. It is through thorough understanding of the underlying structure and elements of perspective drawing that a designer can be free to fully express and control the spatial elements of architecture.

Being able to communicate a design to a client is as important as being able to design. Three dimensional drawing is the most direct way of expressing these ideas to the untrained person. Plans and elevations are much more abstract in concept and are harder for the untrained eye to understand. This is a practical foundation for learning to draw in perspective.

The following section provides some basic tools for both understanding; and practicing; the art of perspective drawing, and the embelllishment of the drawing with rendition of materials and objects. They assume a great deal of effort on the part of the learner, and depend on practice, obsesrvation of other, more proficient drafters, and dissection of successful examples of interior architectural drawing. A bibliography is included to facilitate further study.

MULTIVIEW   SINGLE VIEW

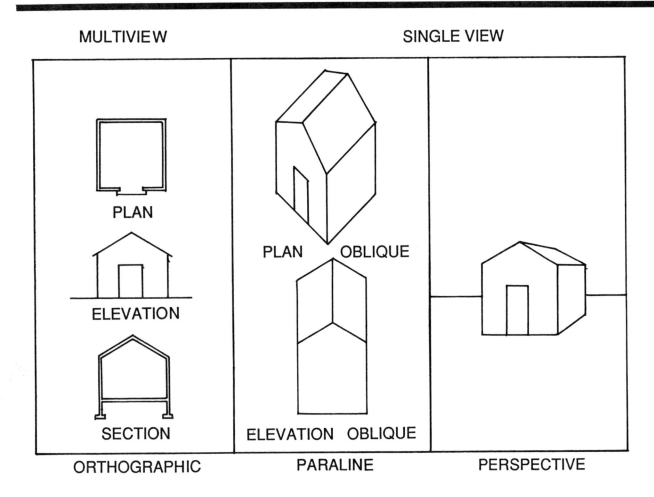

PLAN

ELEVATION

SECTION

PLAN   OBLIQUE

ELEVATION   OBLIQUE

ORTHOGRAPHIC   PARALINE   PERSPECTIVE

SINGLE VIEW DRAWING

In paraline drawings all parallel lines remain parallel rather than
going to a vanishing point as in perspective drawing. In
orthographic drawings it takes more than one view of an object or
scene to give the information as to its three-dimensional shape.
The single view drawings show the spatial relationship in a "single
view." Intrestingly enough the perspective drawing is a 16th century
invention developed by such men as Giovanni Battista Piranesi,
while the more simple multiview drawings are an 18th century
invention.

The isometric is usually based on a 30⁰x30⁰ angle:

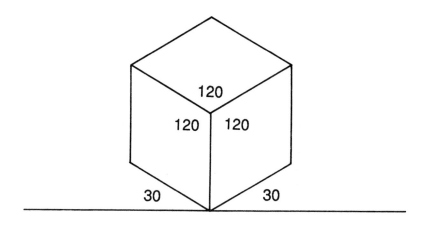

The elevation oblique is usually 45⁰x45⁰ or 30⁰x 60⁰ angle:

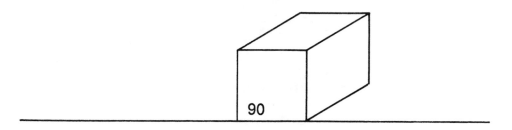

In this case the actual plan is drawn and the verticle lines are lifted from it. The elevation oblique is similar but, in this case, the actual elevation is drawn and the mass behind it is projected back from it.

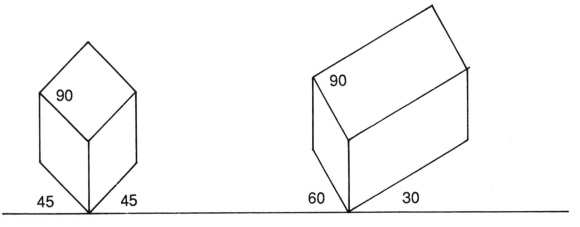

In paraline drawings the measurements are always actual and can be measured with a scale rule. This is a simple, fast way of showing interior scale or a measured three-dimensional object. It is much quicker than perspective but it looks very distorted compared to real life and the perspective conventions. Circles in paraline drawings become elipses and can be drawn easily with inexpensive plastic templates available in many sizes. Non-parallel lines can be found by construction from the measured parallel lines.

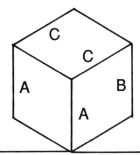

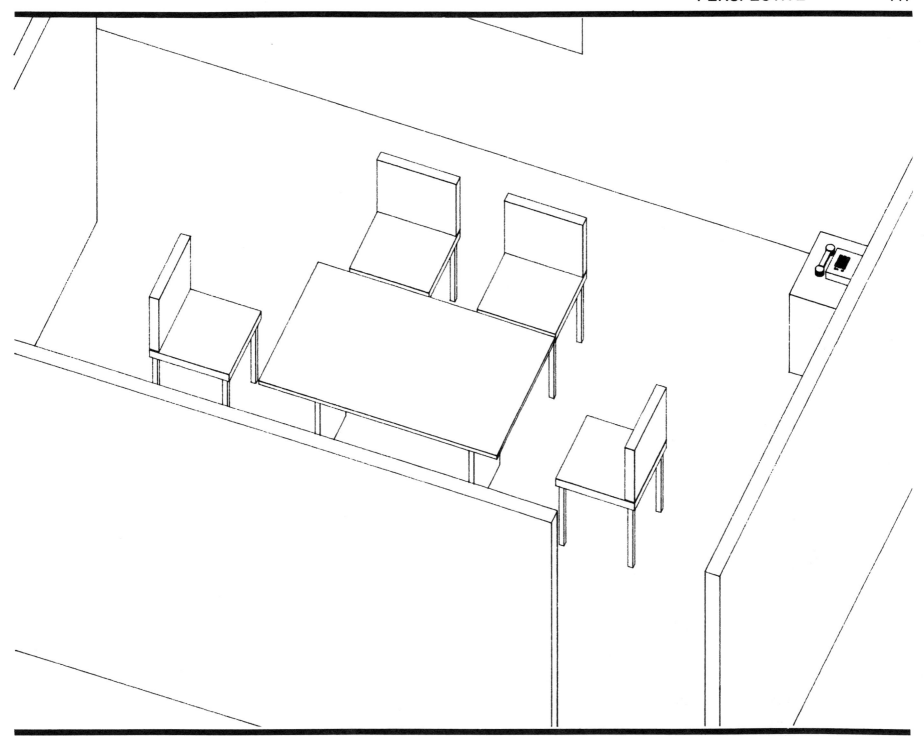

DIMINISHING OF SIZE

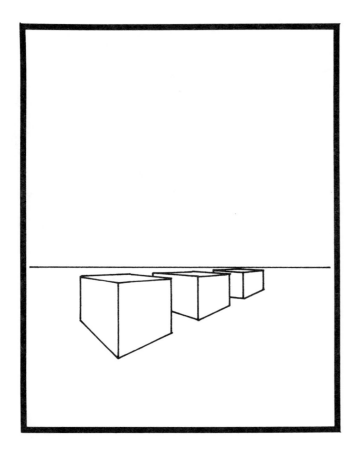

PERSPECTIVE

In perspective drawing we represent in two dimesions a three-dimensional object or scene. There are four basic elements that contribute to the illusion of three-dimensional space.   These elements are 1. diminishing of size;   2. foreshortening; 3. convergence of parallel lines and 4. overlapping of forms.

FORESHORTENING

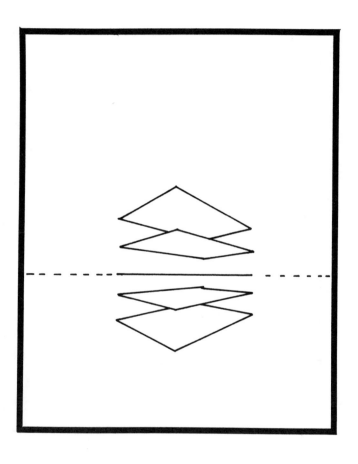

CONVERGENCE OF PARALLEL LINES

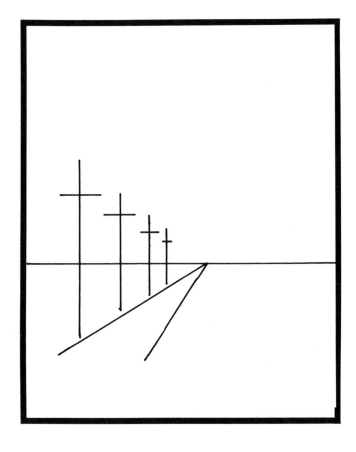

OVERLAPPING OF FORM

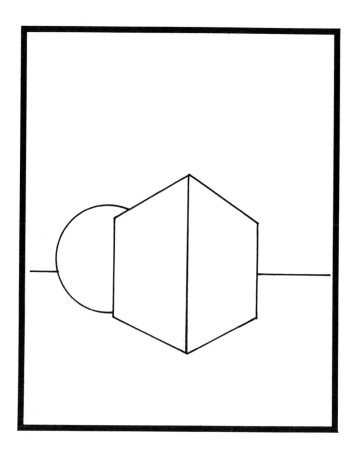

TYPES OF PERSPECTIVE

ONE POINT PERSPECTIVE: The convention where the view or object is placed with its major plane parallel to the picture plane. Good for simple interior drawings.

✗ VP

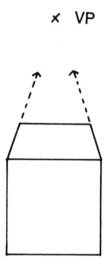

ONE POINT PERSPECTIVE

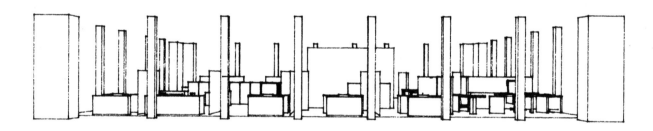

TWO POINT PERSPECTIVE: In two point perspective the major
verticle lines or edges of the object are parallel to the picture plane
but not most sides. This convention is also good for   interior
drawings.

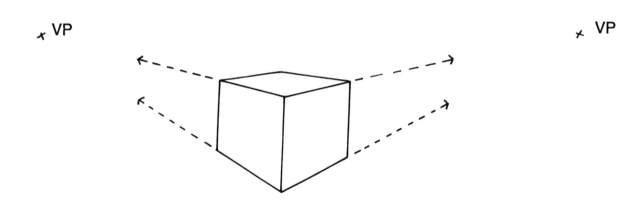

TWO POINT PERSPECTIVE

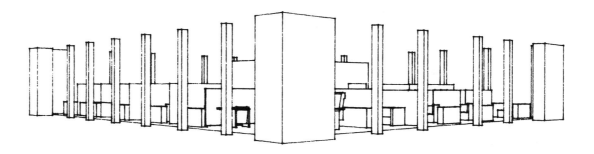

THREE POINT PERSPECTIVE: Occurs when none of the major planes or edges of the object or scene are parallel to the picture plane. This convention is seldom used for interior views because it is less likely to represent a real life view. It is typically used for ground level views of exterior sky scrapers, etc.

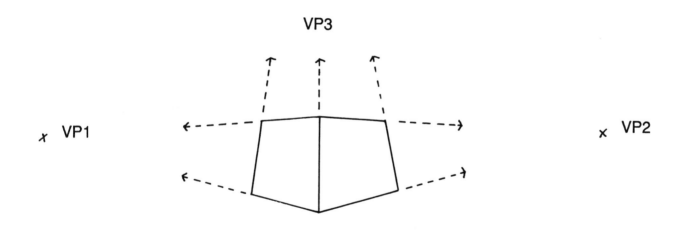

THREE POINT PERSPECTIVE

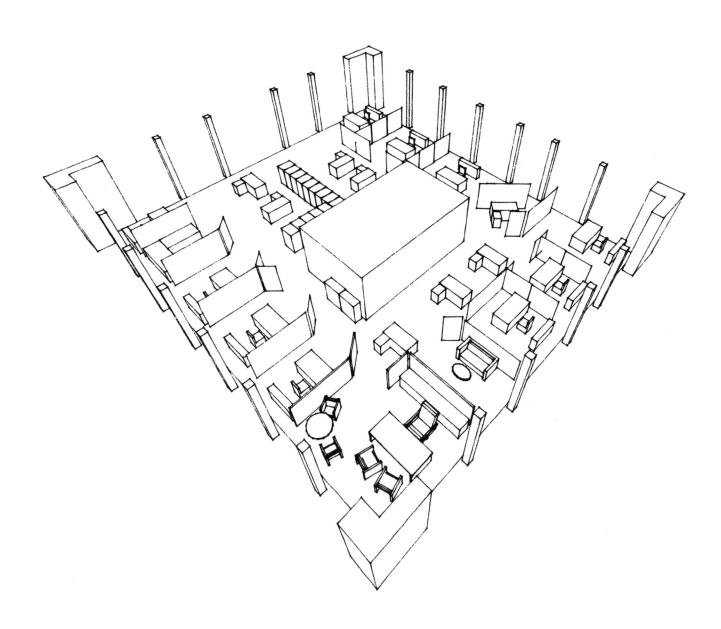

GLOSSARY OF PERSPECTIVE TERMINOLOGY:

OBSERVER POINT (OP):   The position on which the observer stands or sits to view the scene. Also called the Station Point (SP). This position effects the effect of the drawing.

CONE OF VISION: The angle that encompasses the view of the observer, usually 45º-60º. The important elements of the drawing should be within this cone of vision.

CENTER OF VIEW: The point where the observer point is projected into the picture plane.

PICTURE PLANE (PP): The two-dimension plane that the observer sees through. It is perpendicular to the observer's sight line and all lines from the observer to the object cross through it.

GROUND LINE (GL): The intersection of the ground plane and the picture plane. It is used as a measuring line.

GROUND PLANE (GP): This is the floor or ground of the scene. All vertical measures refer to this.

HORIZON LINE: The line that runs paralled to the ground line and intersects the center or the view on the picture plane.   This corresponds to the eye-level of the observer. In interior perspective it is usually five or five and one- half feet above the ground line.

VANISHING POINTS: The point to which all parallel lines converge. All sets of parallel lines have their own vanishing point. In perspective drawing we establish vanishing points for 1, 2 and 3 point presentation but, in fact, there are an infinite number of actual vanishing points.

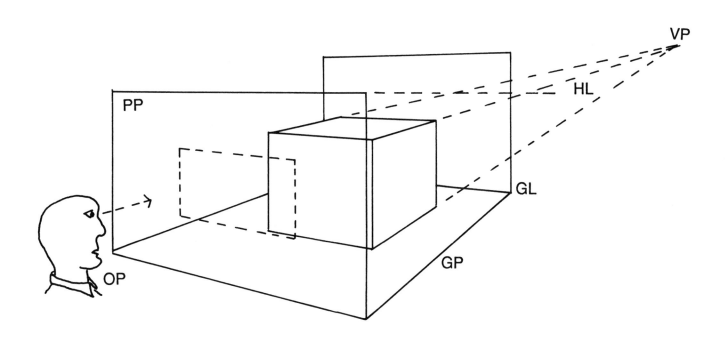

VIEW POINTS

The observer point and the horizon line make the major determination about the effect of the view.

Here the observer gets higher and higher. The further away an observer gets from the picture plane, the flatter the view gets. Also, the position of the picture plane in relationship to the view effects the image.

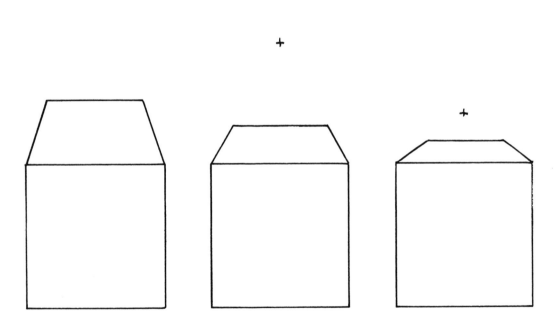

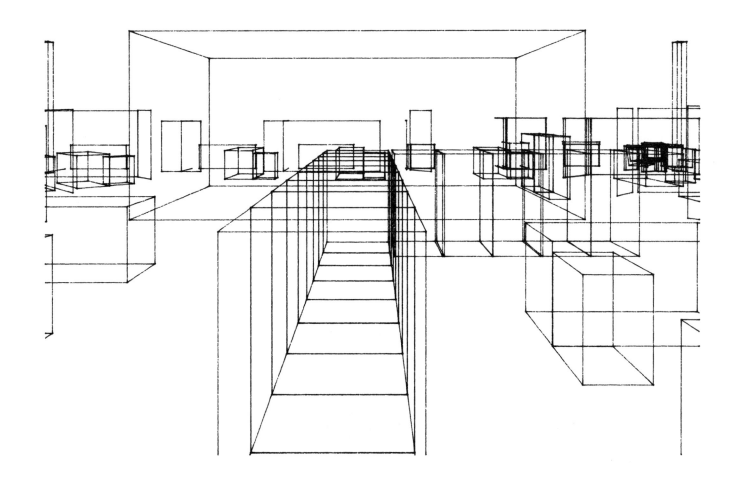

ONE POINT PERSPECTIVE

This system of one point perspective lets you construct a grid of an interior space on which you can draw the furnishings and finishes. The first thing you must do is draw the design in plan form to scale (usually 1/2" or 1/4" for interior views). It is also helpful to draw elevations of the walls and major pieces of furniture. This is particularly helpful to beginners. After you have determined what the space will be:

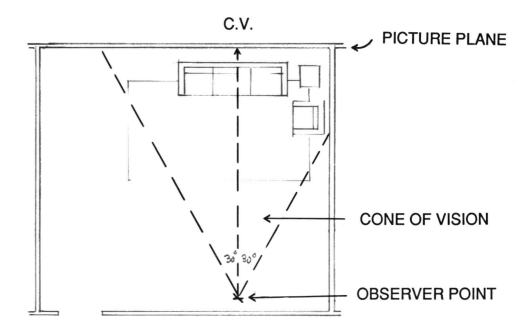

C.V.

PICTURE PLANE

CONE OF VISION

OBSERVER POINT

1.   First, you must determine the observer point in the room. It should be a place from which, if you were standing there, you would be viewing the major elements you wish to illustrate. A useful rule of thumb is to place the observer point twice the distance away from the picture plane as you wish floor to be displayed.   In other words, if you wish to view 12 feet of floor the observer point should be 24 feet from the picture plane.

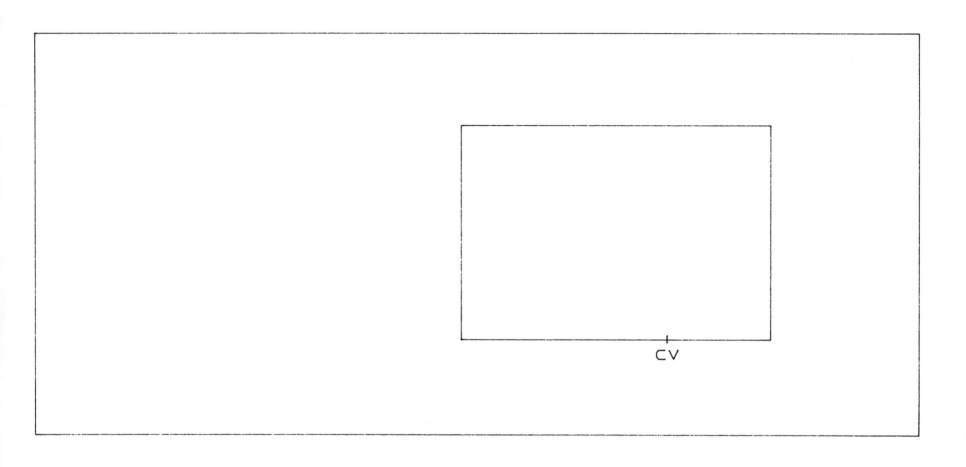

CV

2.   Draw the overall size of the back wall in elevation. This will
be the picture plane.

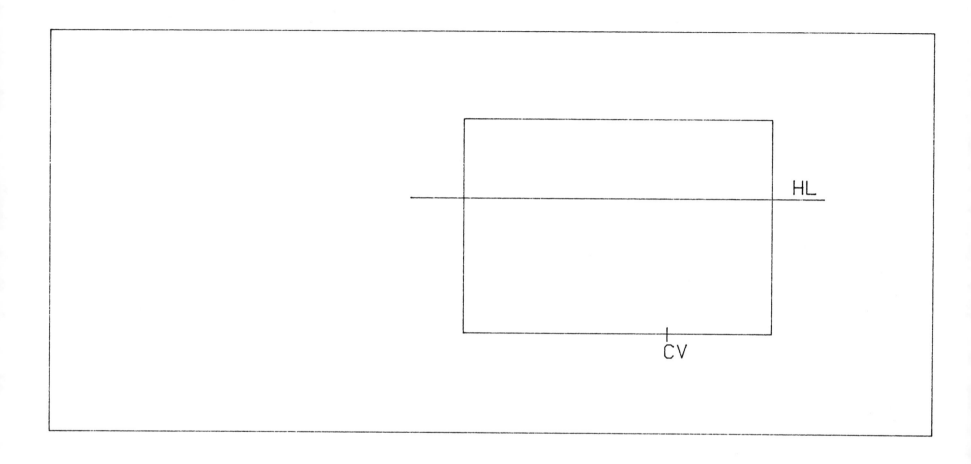

HL

CV

3. Locate the center of vision on the ground line.

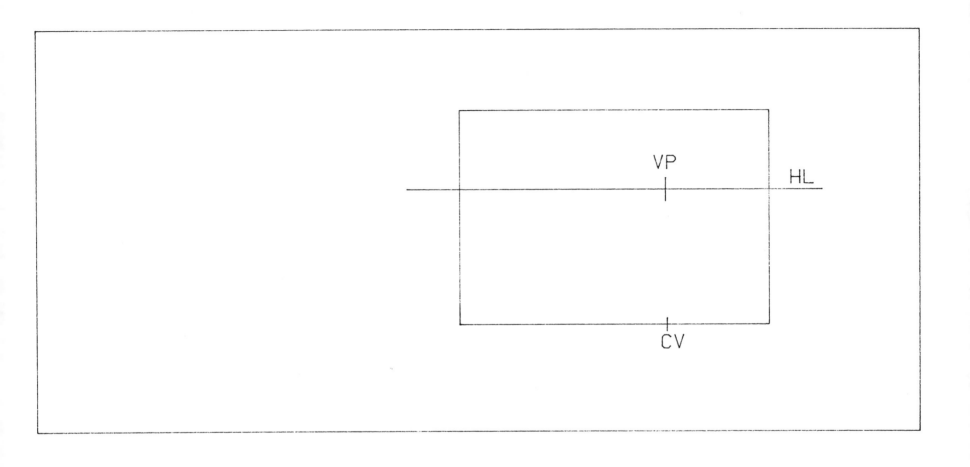

4.   Draw the horizon line 5 feet above the ground line and parallel to it.

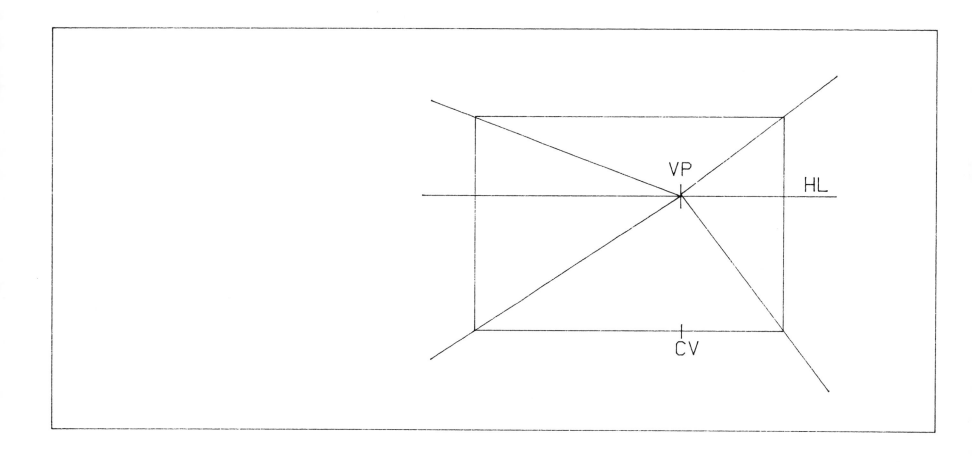

5.   Mark the vanishing point on the horizon line directly above the center of vision.

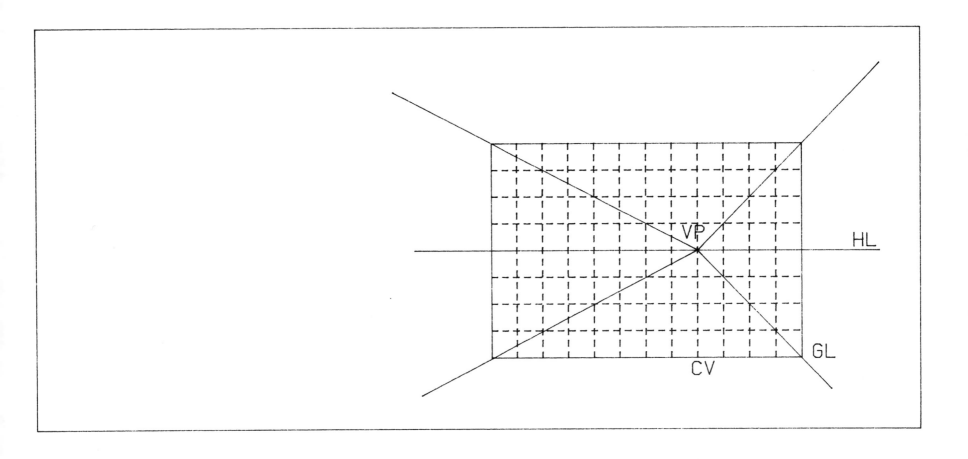

6.   Draw straight lines from the vanishing point through the four
corners of the picture plane.

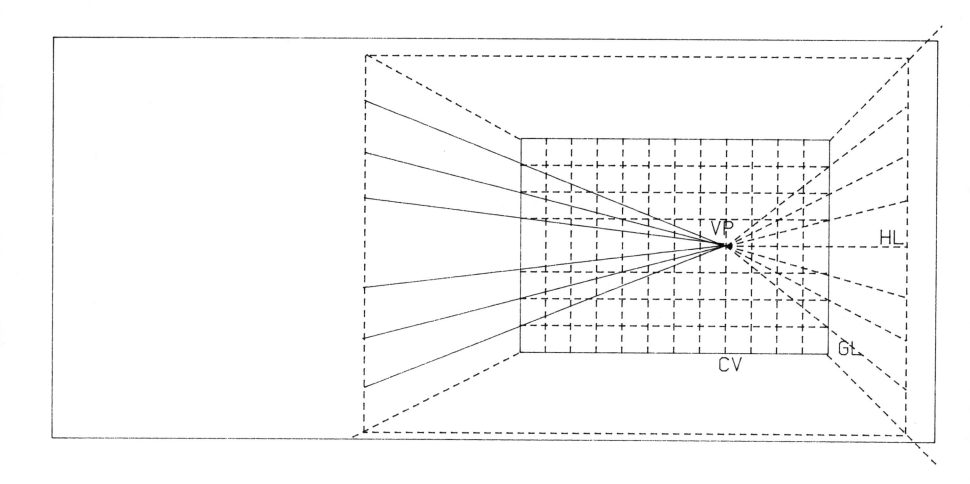

7.   Divide the ground line and the left verticle side of the picture plane into scale with one-foot increments. These   become the measuring lines.

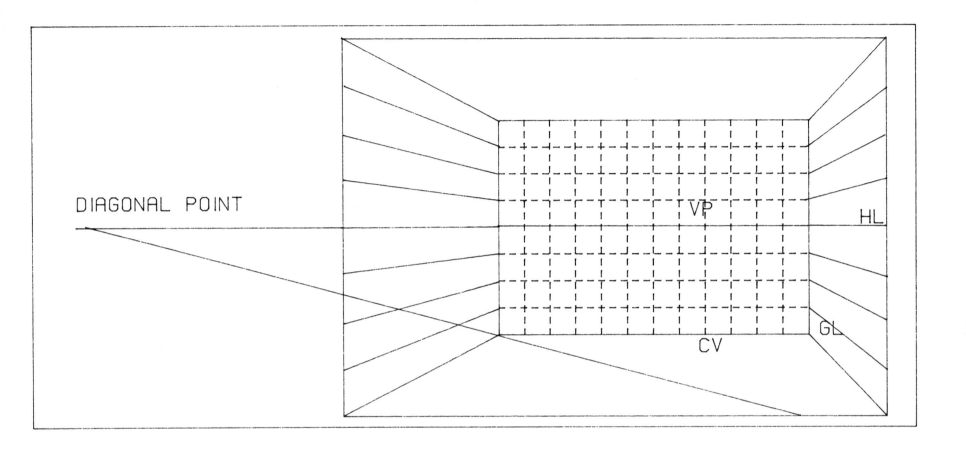

DIAGONAL POINT

VP

HL

GL

CV

8. Draw lines from the vanishing point through each of the one-foot increments.

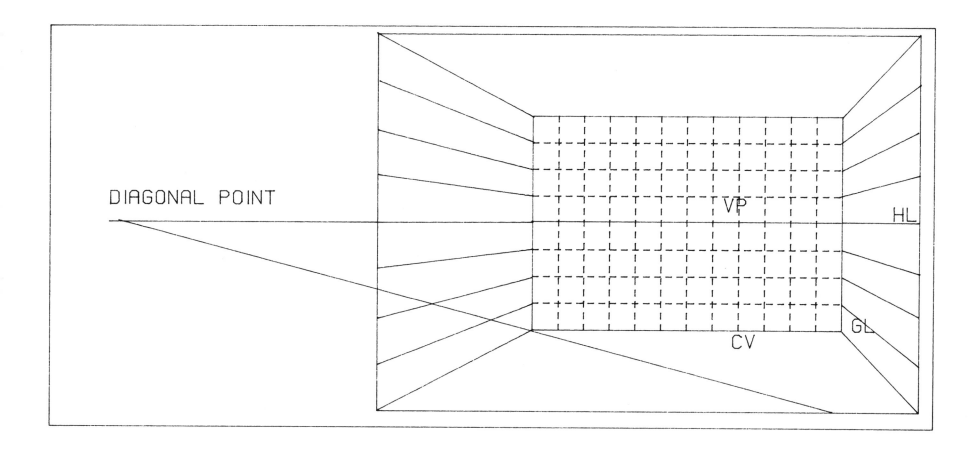

DIAGONAL POINT

VP

HL

GL

CV

9.   Determine what the distance from your observer point to the picture plane wall is (from your plan). Then measure this distance on the horizon line to the left of the vanishing point. This point becomes the Diagonal Point (DP).

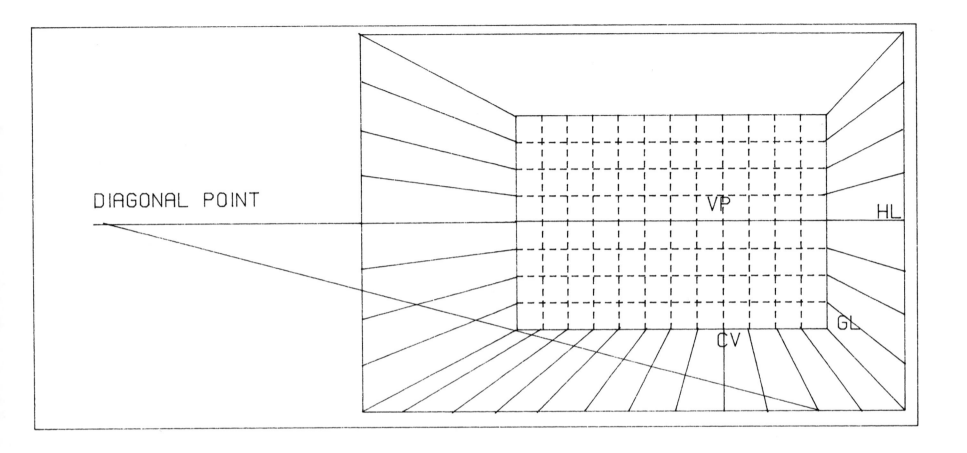

10.   Draw a straight line from the Diagonal Point through the corner of the Picture Plane.

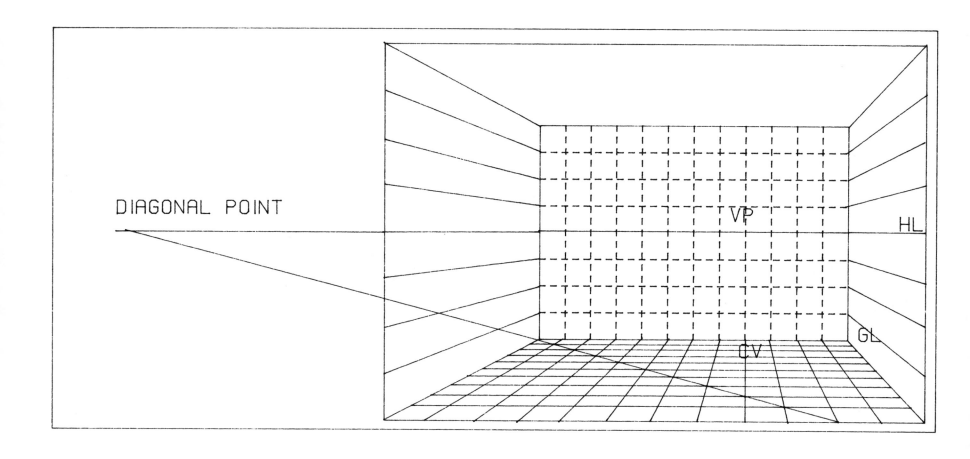

DIAGONAL POINT

VP

HL

CV

GL

11.   Everywhere the Diagonal Line touches a vanishing line, draw a line with your T-Square parallel to the Ground Line.   This establishes 1- foot squares on the floor in perspective.

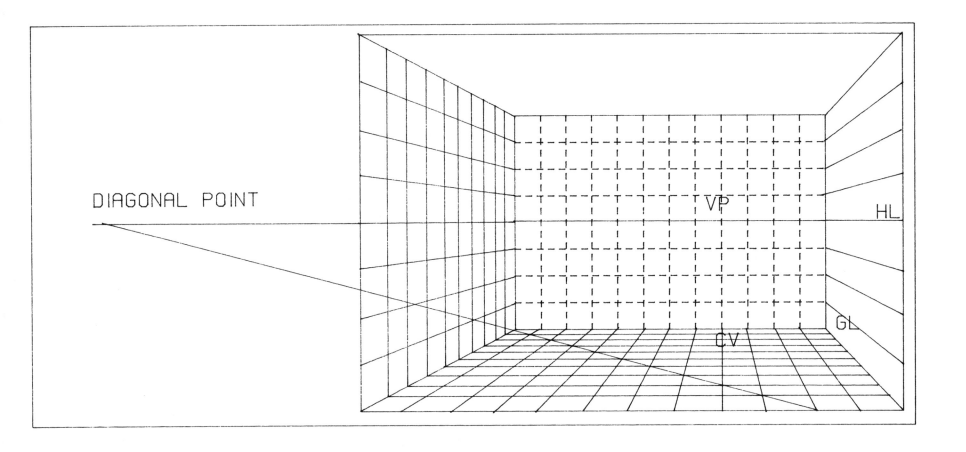

DIAGONAL POINT

VP

HL

CV

GL

12.   Where the constructed horizontal lines on the floor intersect the walls, you may draw verticle lines parallel to the verticle lines on the back wall. This divides the side walls into one-foot squares also.

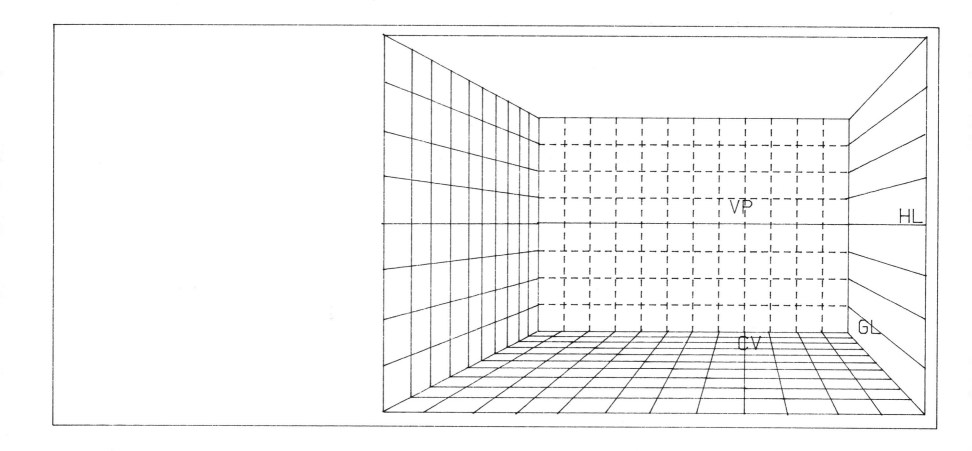

13.   You may also divide the Picture Plane into 1- foot squares.

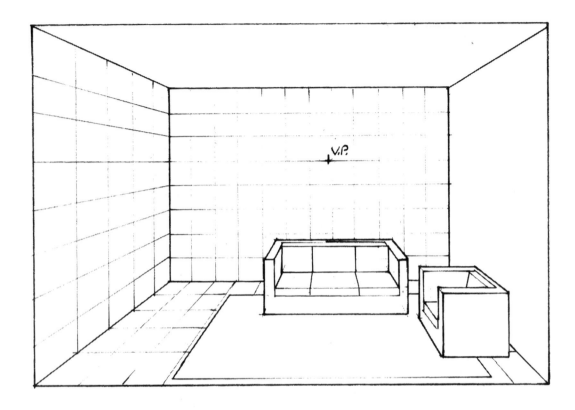

You now have a 1-foot square grid of the exact room you want to draw in perspective. You now may project onto the floor plan you started from. It might be easier to divide your floor plans into 1-foot squares also to give you an orientation and elevation for all your furniture.

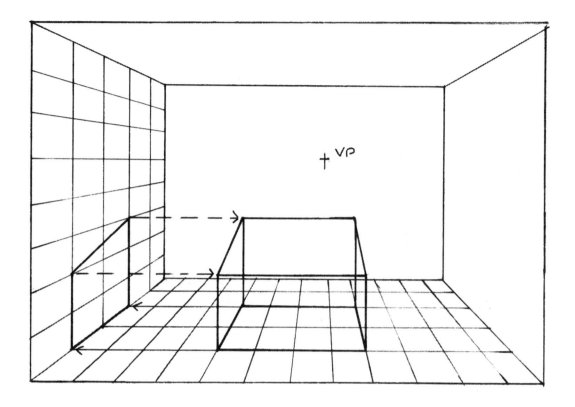

Objects are transferred by the grid method free hand onto the perspective grid. Usually the grid is drawn on tracing paper and then an overlay of tracing paper is taped to the drawing board. The actual perspective drawing is executed on this clean paper, preserving the grid for later use of multiple studies of the same room size and shape. Once the floor plan is projected onto the perspective floor, the vertical elements of the drawing are established.

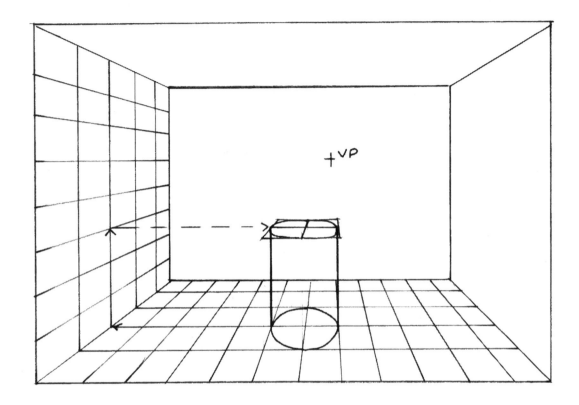

Draw the bottom and top of objects, then connect the sides. You
might also project the elevations of the room or object onto the side
walls, then project them into the center of the room and connect
them down to the plan of the object.

Much of this system depends upon eye/hand practice, carefully looking at the objects you wish to draw, and executing it accurately. Start with simple objects and move to more complex ones as you gain confidence.

This system of grid drawing is quick and simple and can be used for sketches as well as for finished drawings for presentations. There are more complex methods of projecting actual objects and dimensions into perspective. For these systems refer to some of the perspecive books listed in the bibliography. Included here are two, two point perspective grids that can be used in the same manner. Two point perspective "Office Method" projection can also be learned from one of the reference books.

A CIRCLE IN PLAN VIEW

1. Draw a square which will contain the circle.

2. Draw diagonals to position the circle.

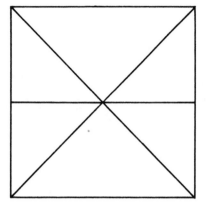

3. Draw a horizontal and verticle line through the center of the square.

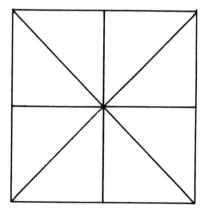

4. Divide half of one diagonal into three equal parts. Select line 1 to 2.

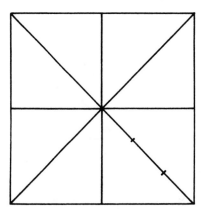

5. Draw a second square in the first, starting from point 3. The sides should be parallel to the sides of the first square.

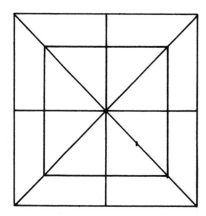

6. Use the eight points you have now constructed to draw, freehand, a circle within the square.

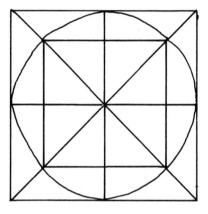

A CIRCLE IN PERSPECTIVE

1.First draw a two-foot square in your perspective grid. Then divide it diagonally.

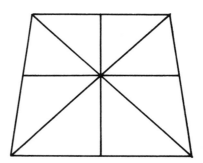

2. Divide one of the diagonal lines into three equal parts.

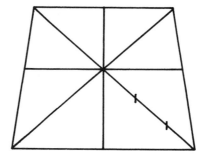

3. Draw a second perspective square as you did in the plan view square.

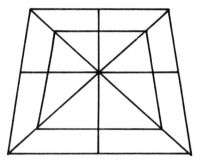

4. To conclude, Draw a freehand cirdle using the constructed guide points. Make sure you practice this, it is easy to include distortion in the circle.

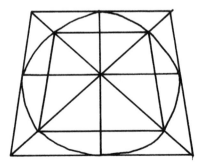

SHADES AND SHADOWS

Standard exterior shadows are simply rendered at a 45º degrees.

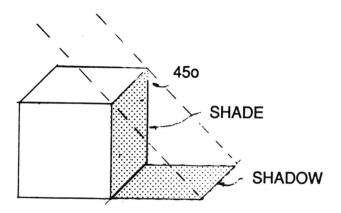

The shadow is then cast on the ground. The side opposite the light source is then in shade.

The shadow conforms to the countour of the surface it falls on.

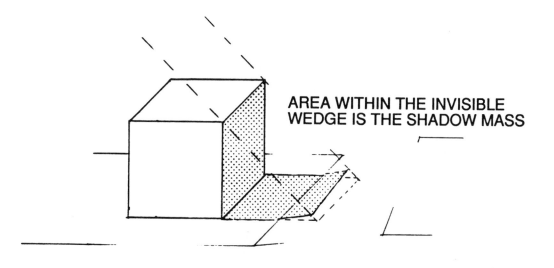

The object interferes with the shadow mass and the shadow climbs up the object until it is outside the shadow mass and is the illuminated by the light source.

Shadows are parallel to the line making the shadow when the line is parallel to the plane on which it falls.
Interior shadows are slightly different because they are closer to the point source than to the sun.

Light from a ceiling source would splay out from the point directly beneath the source on the floor. If the source was the sun or a window (large source) or skylight (large source) the edges of the shadow would be parallel rather than splayed.

Shade and shadows are simple in principle but complex in application. For much more detailed explanations and examples refer to one of the excellent books listed in the bibliorgaphy.

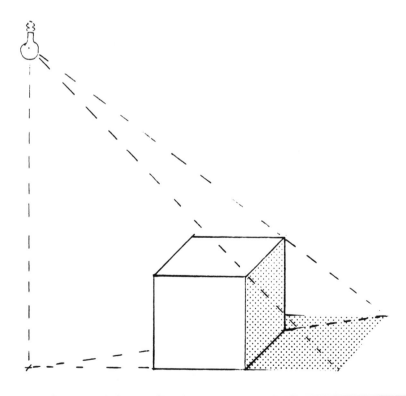

TWO POINT PERSPECTIVE

The two point perspective grid is used in the same way as the one-point grid. The only additional complication is the use of both vanishing points in constructing objects within the grid. Drawing with the grid itself, however, is self evident. When you are drawing objects use the same construction techniques that you learned when drawing the grid itself. Now lets make the two point grid.

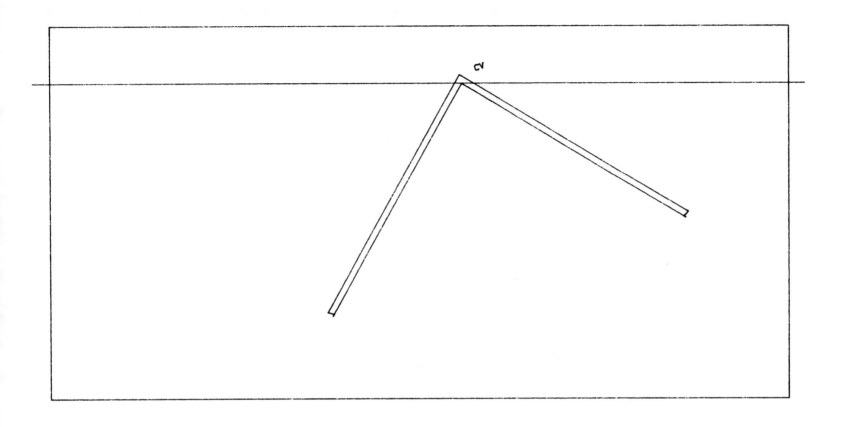

CONSTRUCTING A TWO POINT GRID

1.   Draw plan to scale and determine observer point and line of vision.

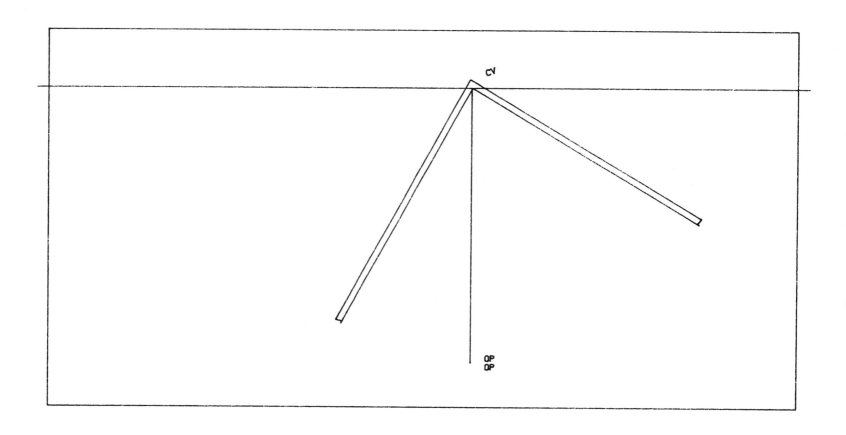

2.   The Picture Plane will touch the furthest corner of your wall. The Picture Plane is perpendicular to the observer Lines of Vision. Your vertical measuring line occurs where the corner touches the Picture Plane.

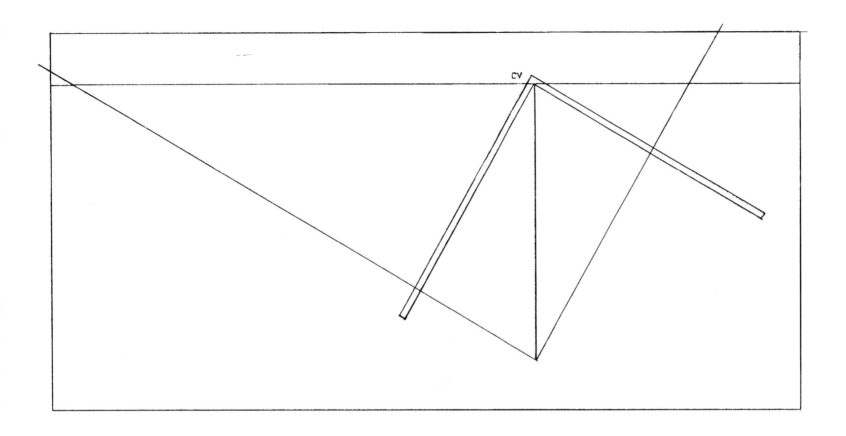

3.   From the Observer Point draw a line parallel to the left wall.
Where this intersects the Picture Plane the vanishing point right
(VPR) occurs. Draw a line from the OP parallel to the right wall,
and where this line intersects the PP the VP left occurs.

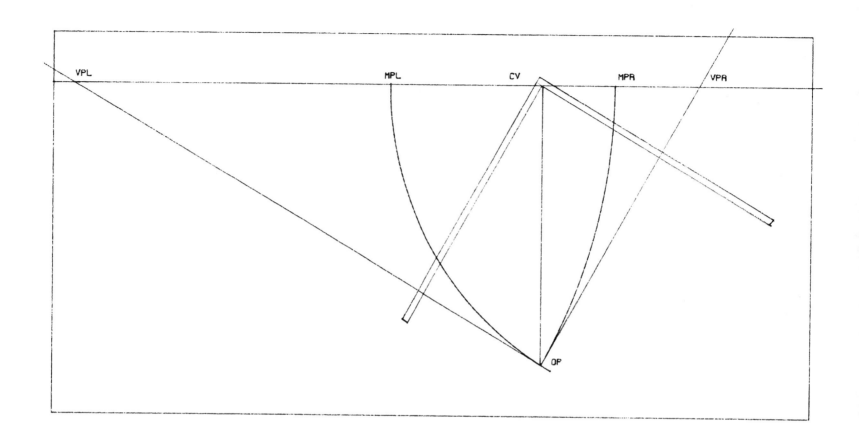

4. Measure the distance from the VPL to the OP. Now measure along the PP from the VPL the same distance to the right, and this mark becomes the measuring point right (MPR). The distance from OP to VPR to the left of VPR on the PP will give the MP Left.

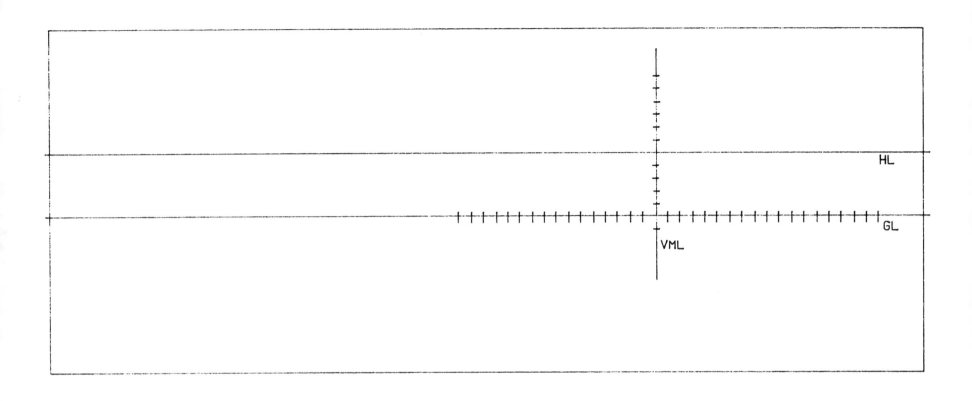

5.   Now we can begin to construct our two point perspective grid on our paper. First, draw a ground line (GL) parallel to the bottom edge of the paper. Now draw a vertical measuring line (VML) perpendicular to the ground line. Next, divide your ground line and vertical measuring line into one foot increments at any scale appropriate for your paper size. Now locate the observer eye level on the VML, and through this point draw your horizon line (HL) parallel with the ground line.

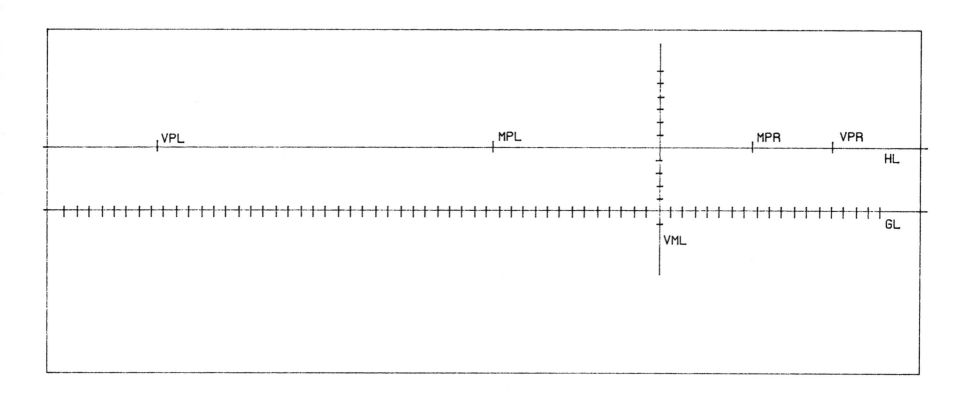

6.   Mark on you horizon line the VPL, MPL, MPR, VPR, CV, using the measurement arrived at on your plan layout. (This need not be at the same scale, but the measurements should correlate.)

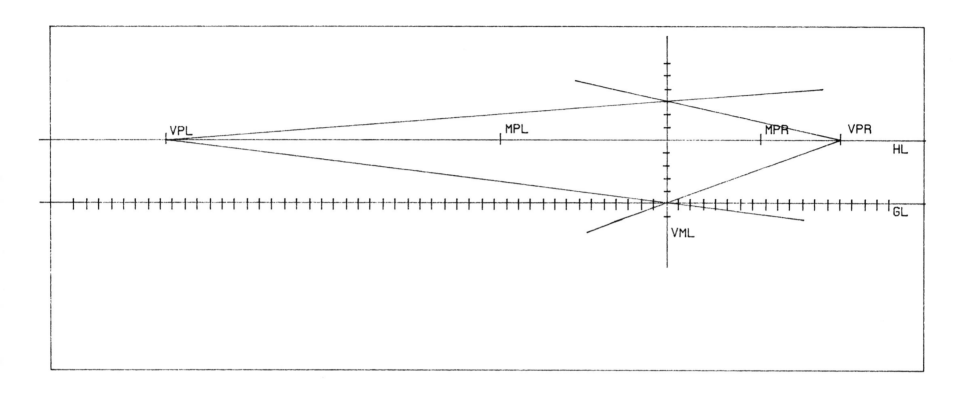

7. From the left and right vanishing points draw lines through the point where the ground line intersects the VML. This gives us the major baselines. Also draw lines from your vanishing points through the ceiling height on your VML. This gives your ceiling lines.

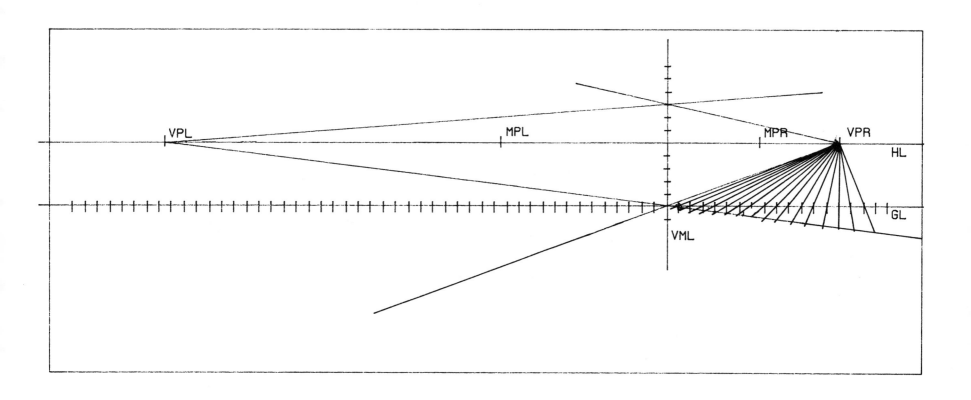

8. From the left and right measuring points draw through the 1'
marks on your ground line until they intersect your major base lines
below your GL.

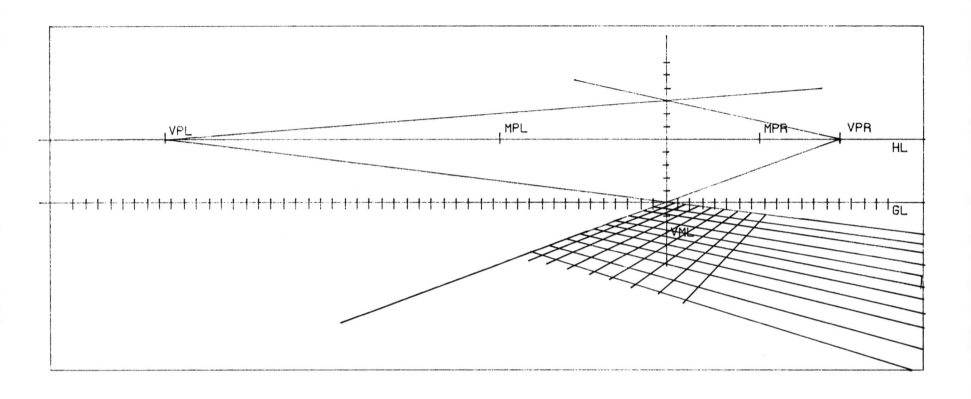

9.   You have now gridded off your two point perspective floor in one foot squares. Now draw vertical lines parallel to the VML from the intersection of your one foot marks on you major base lines until they intersect your wall top lines.

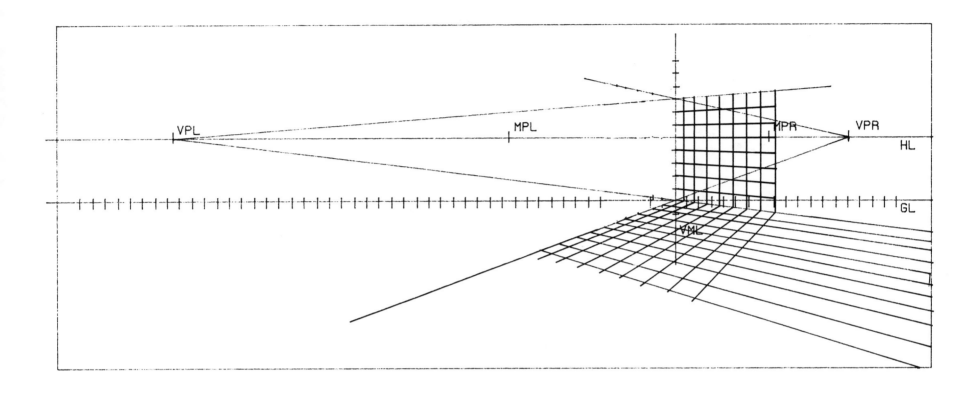

10.   Finally, draw lines from your VPL and VPR through the VML, and from your GL to the wall top. This will grid the walls into one foot squares. You now have a complete room perspective grid customized to your chosen point of view and dimension.

You may now use the same system of drawing objects in the space you used in your one point grid. The only difference is that lines parallel to the left wall recede to the VPR and vice versa.

RENDERING & ENTOURAGE

The scope of this chapter is to provide an introduction to black and white drawing and rendering techniques. Color rendering is another matter and there are several classic books listed in the bibliography.

Aside from paper and drafting tools, the most important tools in the renderer's kit are pencils and ink pens. Most designers use the all-purpose drawing pencil (graphite) in F, 4B, 2H, B, AND 2B grades for most drawings. The *Prismacolor* or *Verithin* black wax pencil is also popular and quite effective on all paper types. The third major tool is the technical pen such as *Rapidograph* and *Technos*, filled with india ink, in 00, 000, 0, 1 and 2 1/2 size points for most drawing needs. The most popular sketching tool is the felt tip pen in various brands and is probably today's most used quick-sketch tool.

Most design quick-sketching is done on yellow roll tracing paper or white bond. The tracing paper allows many overlays as the designer thinks and develops ideas. Only small areas can be changed at a time and the entire sketch can quickly be traced saving much time. The dominant medium for finished black and white drawings is a vellum tracing paper such as *Clearprint* or *Albanene*. Some designers prefer to work on Mylar. The tracing media allows easy and inexpensive reproduction on *Diazo* prints that can quickly be colored with pencil or felt tip pens for presentation and studies.

The only way to learn rendering is by steady practice and constant study of other people's drawing, and the materials themselves. The renderer must learn to look at the actual material and simplify it into credible symbols. The standard architectural symbols can quickly be learned from study, copying the examples included in this section, tracing and by adaption. Never hesitate to trace from magazines, photos, your own Polaroid shots, and constantly adapt them for you own use. Furniture catalogues are great for furniture and the Sears' Catalogue is a treasure house of clippings. The examples of people, furniture and other entourage included here are from *Entourage, A Tracing File* by Ernest Burden and *A Graphic Vocabulary for Architectural Presentation* by Edward T. White, both highly recommended books.

In developing interior design drawings, it is always recommended to include people in the drawing to show scale and vitality. Also include plants, pictures, accessories and lighting effects to help communicate the "ambience" of the finished design.

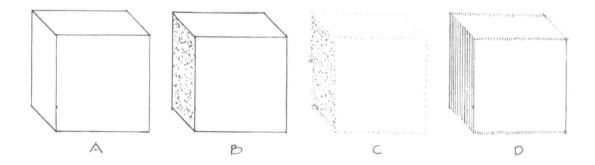

There are four basic types of line rendition techniques: a. Line; b. Line and Tone; c. Pure Tone and d. Tone of Line.

There are other techniques that come in handy for renderings, such as *Zipatone* screens and *Paratone* materials sheets that include pre-printed brick, stone, etc. These are best used in plan and elevation renderings, but can also be effective in perspective drawings.

VALUE/TEXTURE RENDITION

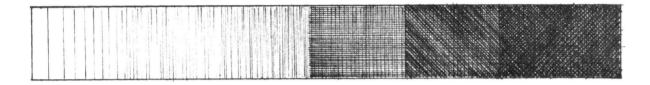

LINE

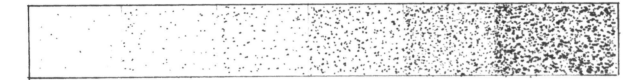

DOT

SCRIBBLE

ZIPATONE

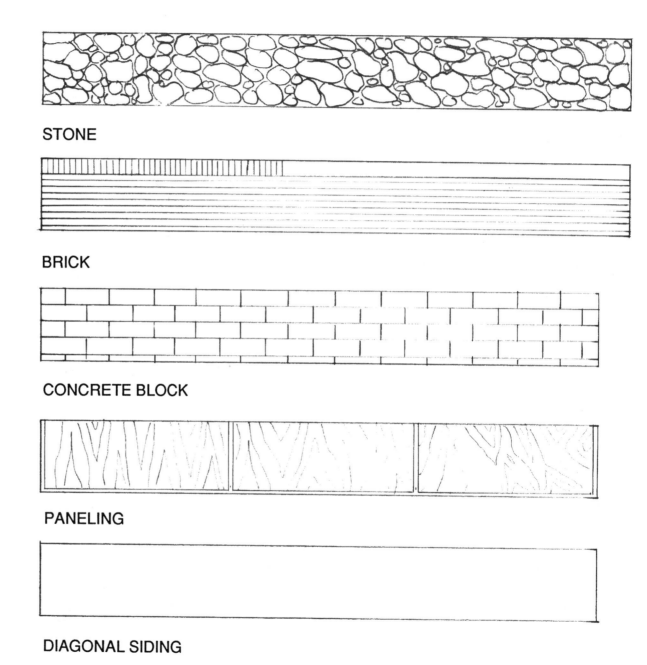

STONE

BRICK

CONCRETE BLOCK

PANELING

DIAGONAL SIDING

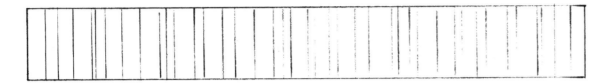

RANDOM SIDING

SHINGLES

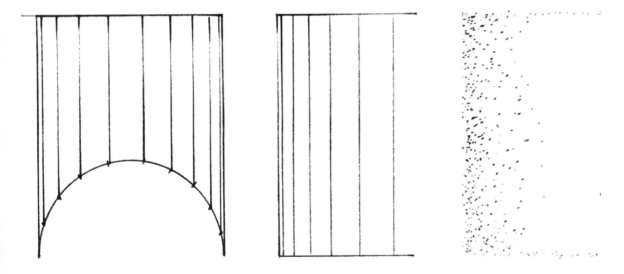

CYLINDERS

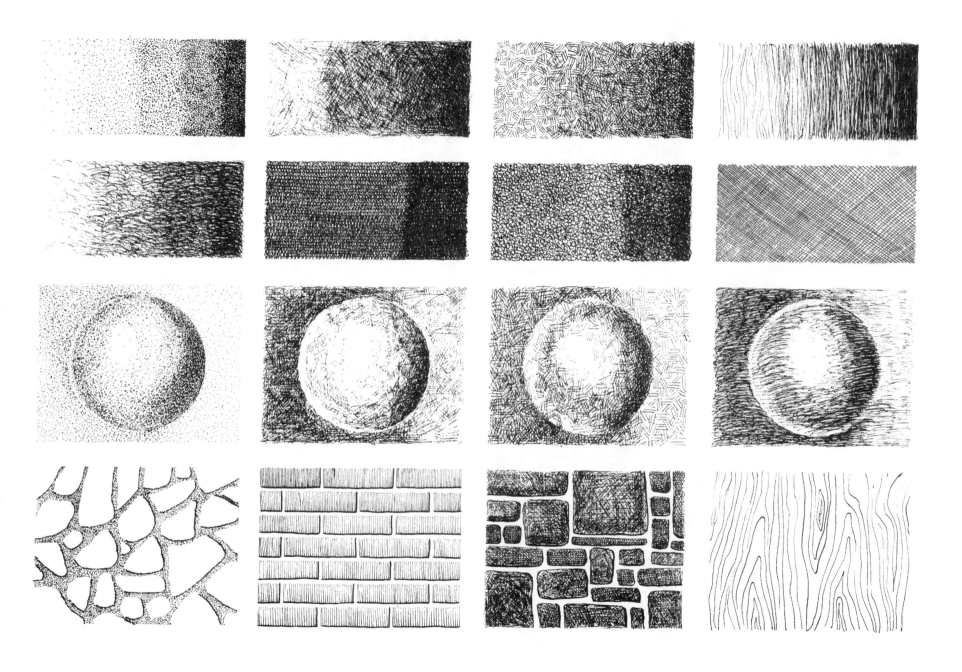

RENDERING EXAMPLES

The following section is an excerpt from an excellent workbook of rendering techniques in pen and ink and an encyclopedia of entourage tools and samples. Entourage is the process of dressing a drawing with people, plants and accessories. The book is *A Graphic Vocabulary for Architectural Presentation* by Edward T. White. It is important to fill out the drawings you make. A drawing does not fully represent an interior space without the things that will occupy it.

The viewer must have a frame of reference to give a realistic sense of scale. People are the most direct way of telegraphing this relationship. Most students and many experienced designers are intimidated with the idea of drawing people. The simplest and best way of overcoming this fear is to use the same technique that professional renderers do, tracing! The people pictures can be traced from magazines, catalogues and photographs, just remember to place the eye level of any standing figures at the horizon line of your drawing.

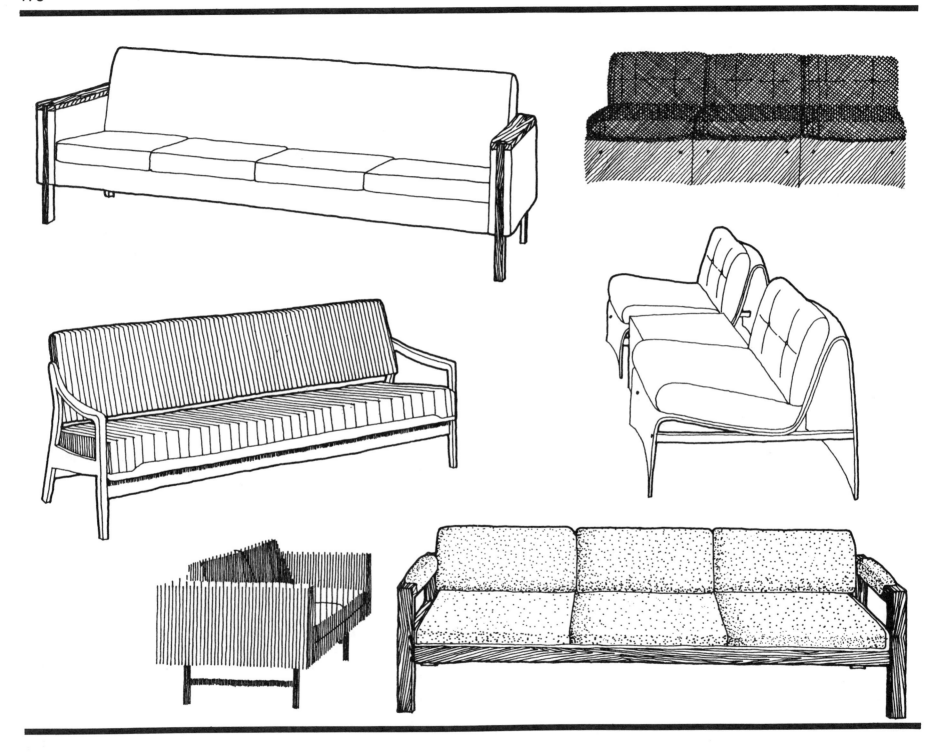

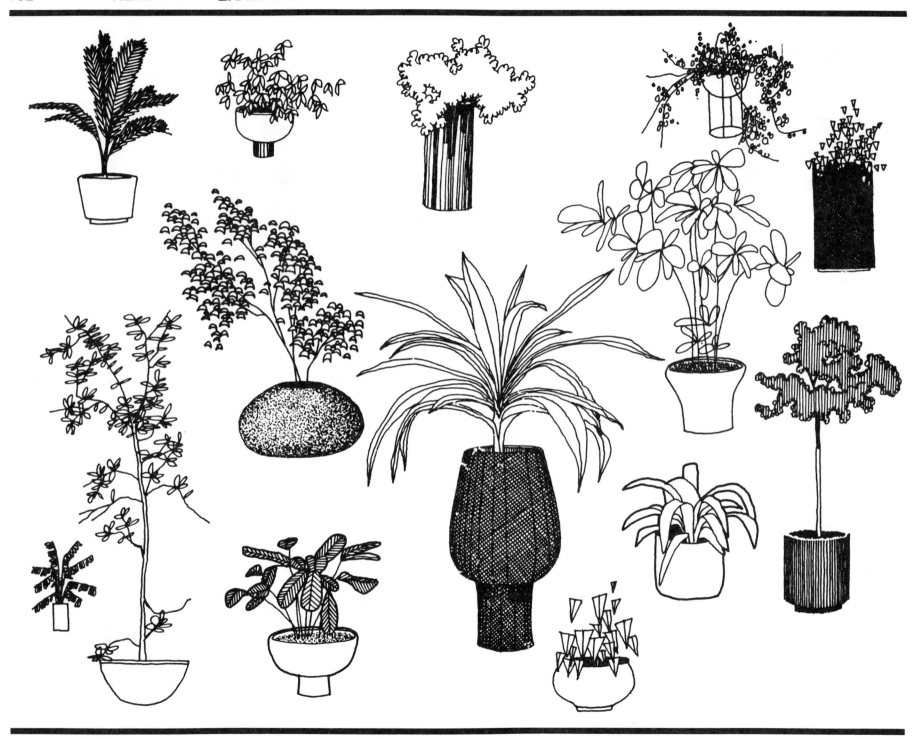

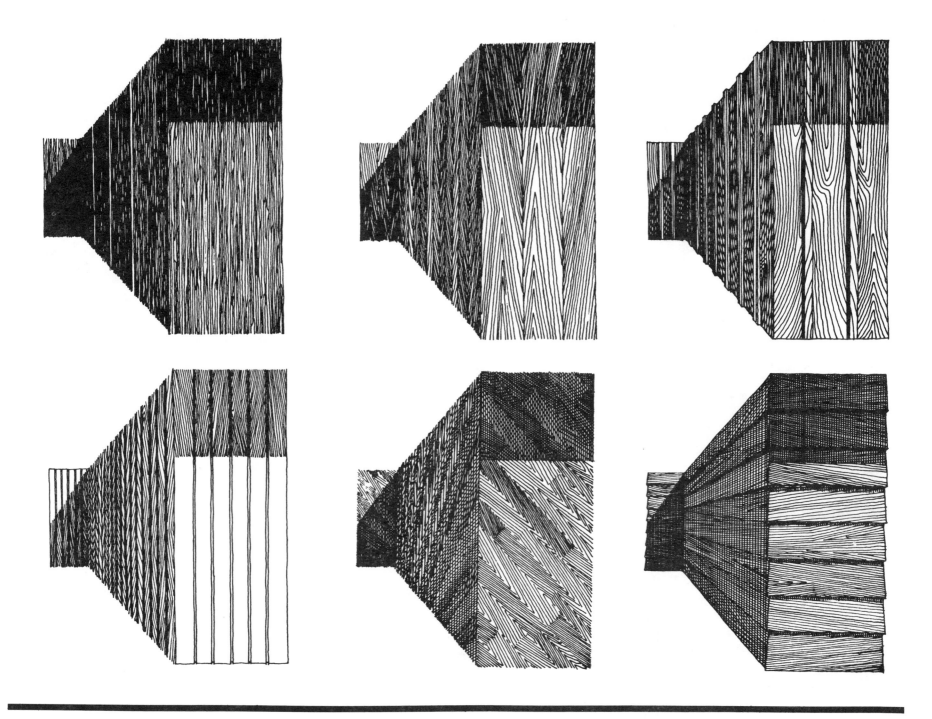

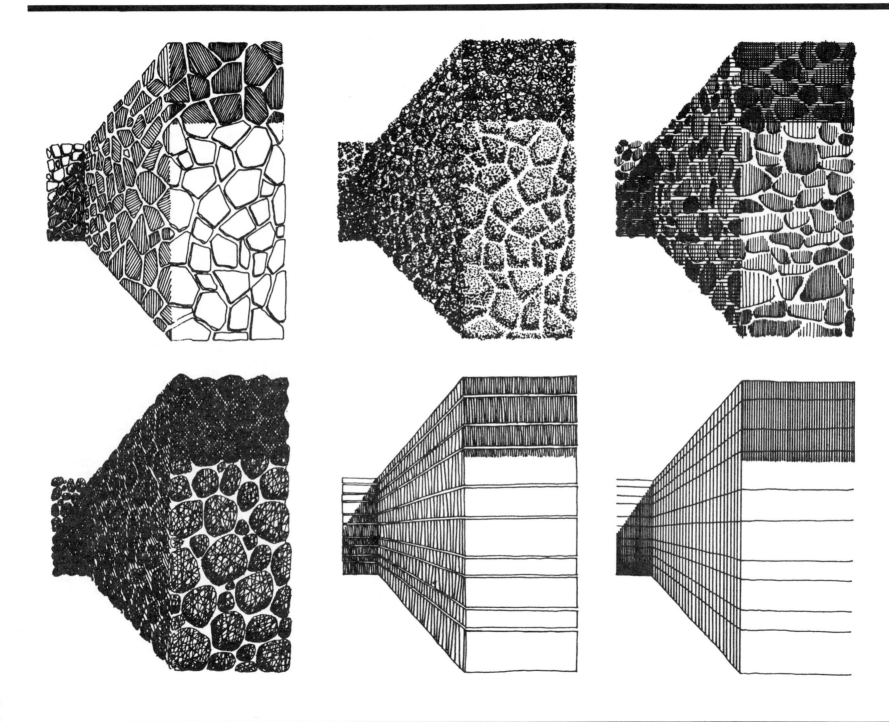

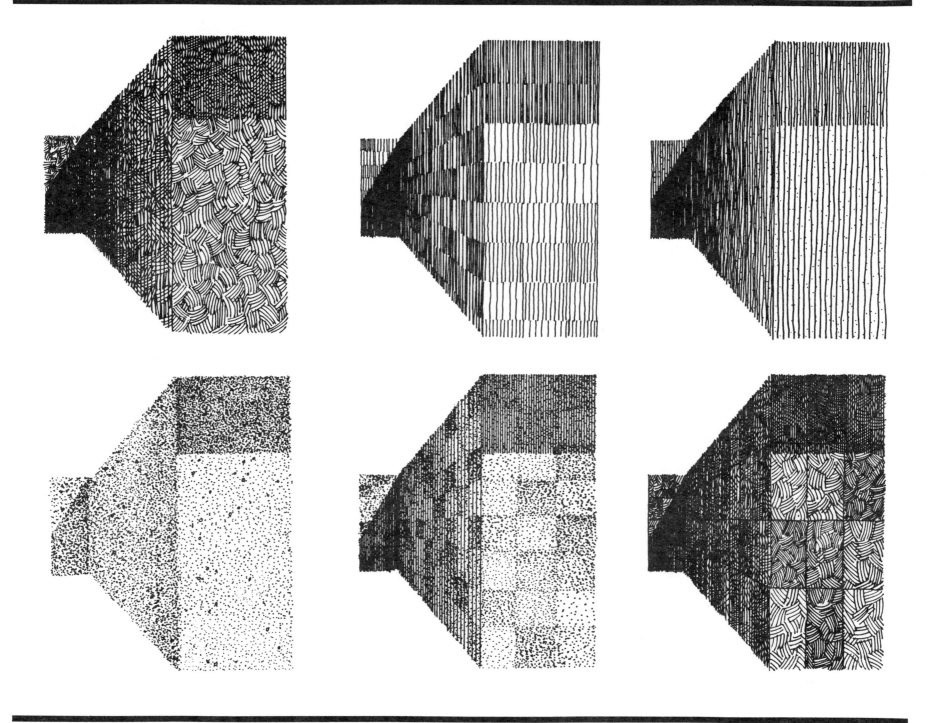

EXAMPLES

Without a doubt the best way to learn how to draft is to do it!   The next best way, and part of the process of "doing it" is to follow the examples of others who have come before us.   This section compiles many examples of professional and student work for you to study.   Use them as guides, idea stimulators, copy book examples, standards and models. Analyze them carefully, but feel free to extablish your own style and methods.   There are always many correct ways of solving the same problem. Your solution may blaze a new graphic trail.

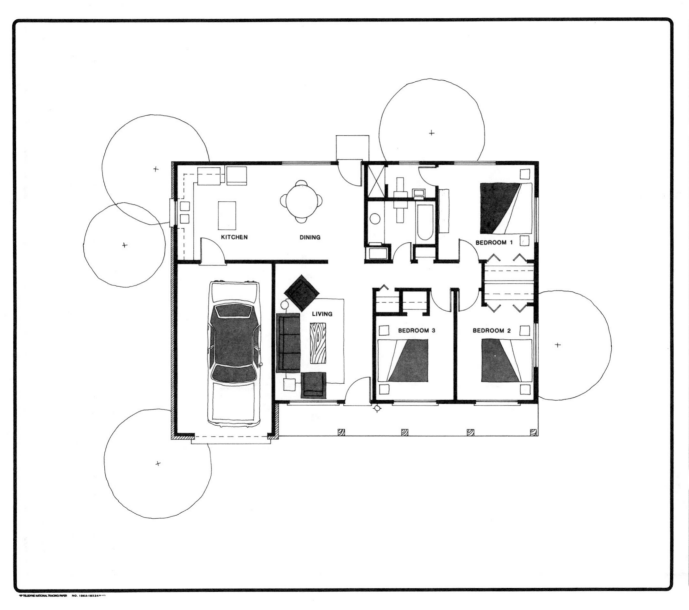

KITCHEN   DINING

BEDROOM 1

LIVING

BEDROOM 3   BEDROOM 2

REVISIONS   BY
5-8-83

FREDERIC JONES DESIGN ASSOCIATES
1500 16TH STREET, SAN FRANCISCO, CALIFORNIA 94103

DRAWN

CHECKED

DATE
4-10-84

SCALE
¼" = 1'-0"

JOB NO.
85-0105

SHEET

OF   SHEETS

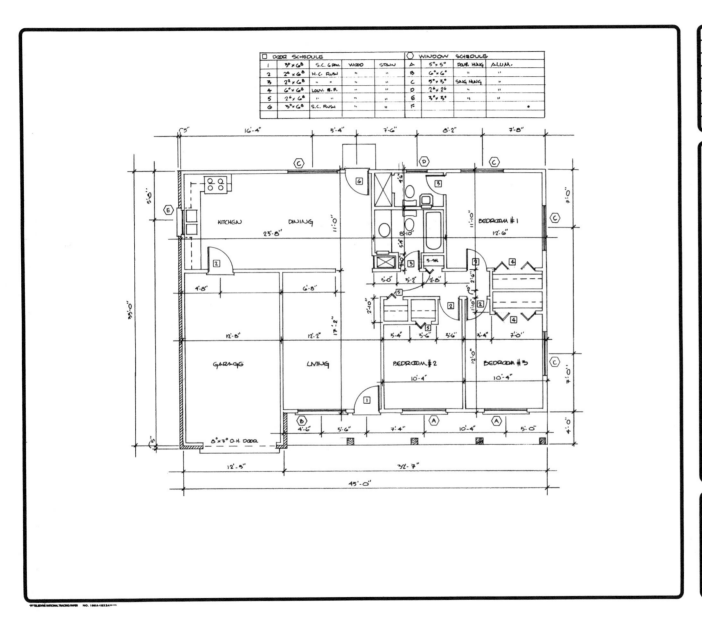

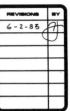

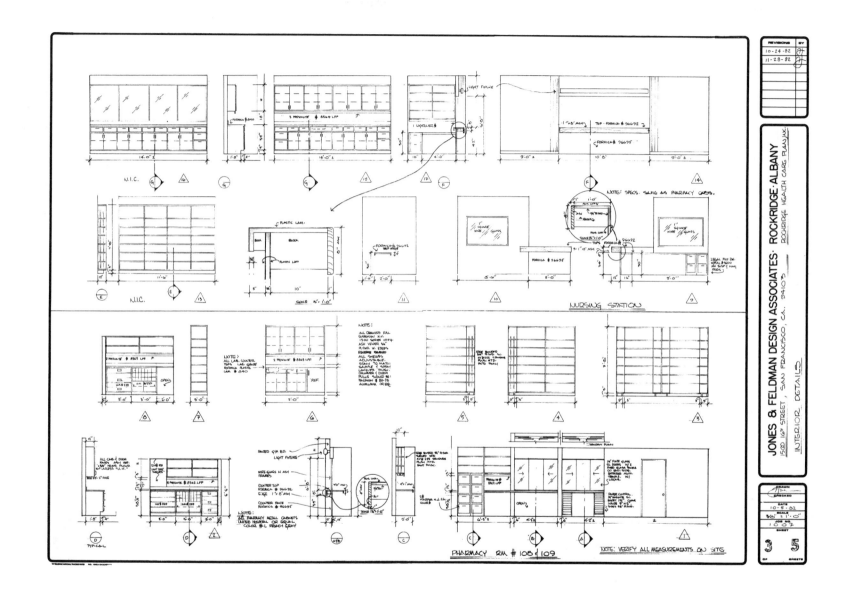

NURSING STATION

PHARMACY RM # 108 & 109

NOTE: VERIFY ALL MEASUREMENTS ON SITE

JONES & FELDMAN DESIGN ASSOCIATES : ROCKRIDGE-ALBANY

ROCKRIDGE HEALTH CARE PLAN, INC.

1500 16TH STREET, SAN FRANCISCO, CA. 94103

INTERIOR DETAILS

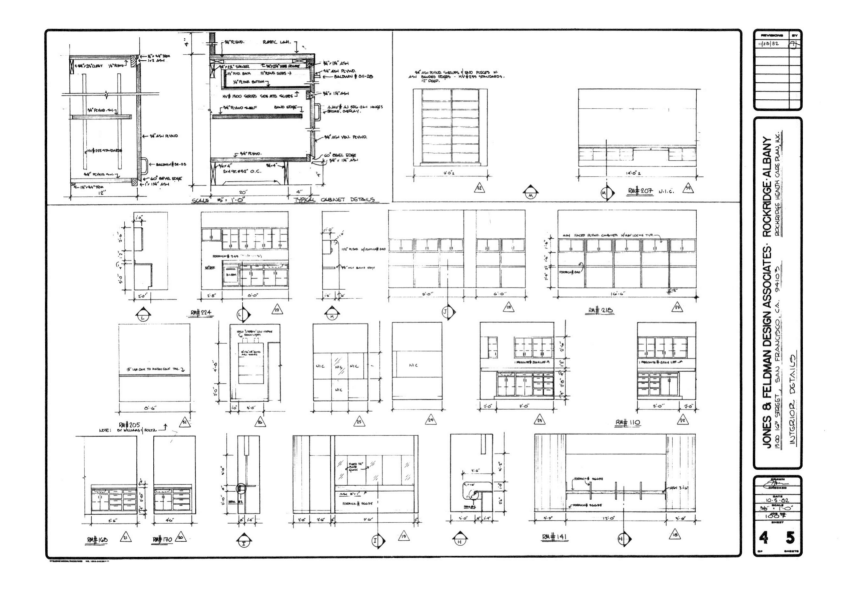

SCALE 3" 1'-0"   TYPICAL CABINET DETAILS

JONES & FELDMAN DESIGN ASSOCIATES · ROCKRIDGE · ALBANY

ROCKRIDGE HEALTH CARE PLAN, INC.

1500 16TH STREET, SAN FRANCISCO, CA. 94103

INTERIOR DETAILS

4 OF 5 SHEETS

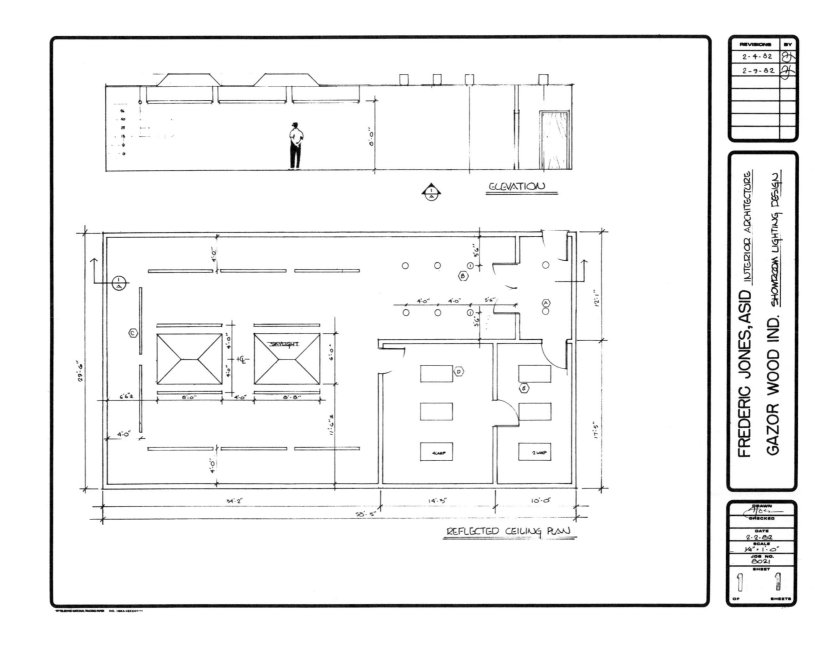

ELEVATION

REFLECTED CEILING PLAN

FREDERIC JONES, ASID INTERIOR ARCHITECTURE
GAZOR WOOD IND. SHOWROOM LIGHTING DESIGN

REVISIONS	BY
2-4-82	
2-9-82	

DRAWN

CHECKED

DATE
2-2-82
SCALE
1/4" = 1'-0"
JOB NO.
8021
SHEET

1 OF   1 SHEETS

WORK STATION STANDARD

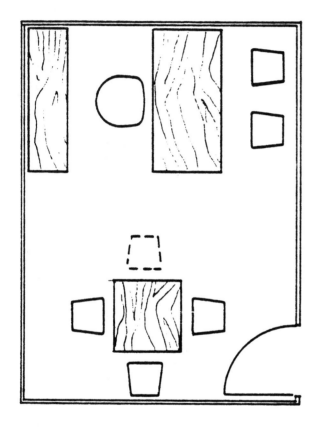

6B

Desk, 36" x 72"
Credenza, 20" x 72"
Visitor Chairs
Conference Table, 36" sq.
Conference Chairs

192 ⬡

6B

WORK STATION STANDARD

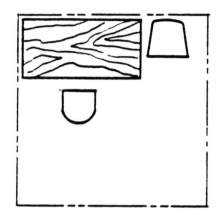

2A

Desk, 30" x 60"

Visitor Chair

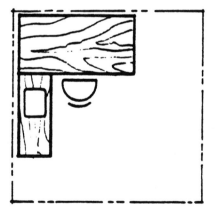

2B

Desk with Return

   30" x 60"
   with 42" Return

64 ⌼

2A,B

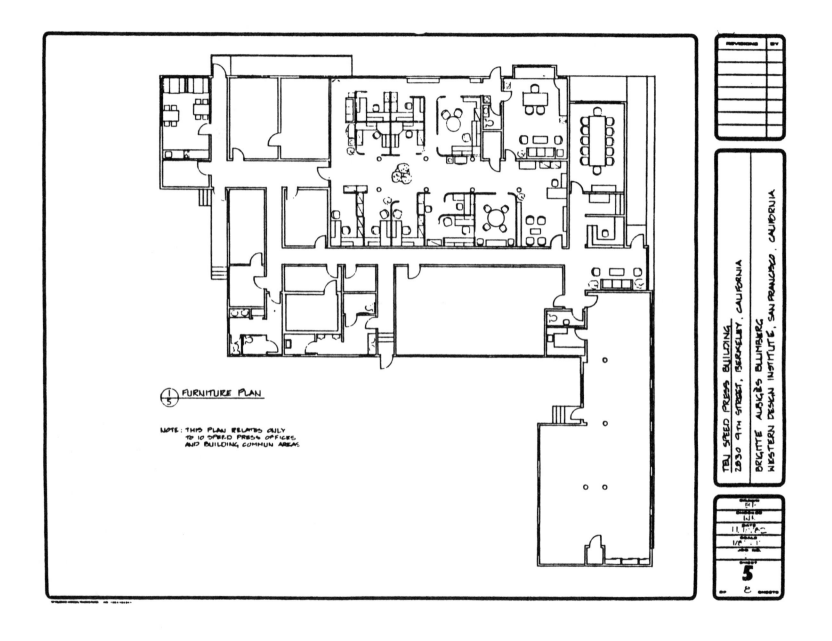

① FURNITURE PLAN
⑤

NOTE: THIS PLAN RELATES ONLY
TO 10 SPEED PRESS OFFICES
AND BUILDING COMMUN AREAS

TEN SPEED PRESS BUILDING
2830 9TH STREET, BERKELEY, CALIFORNIA

BRIGITTE ALISGES BLUMBERG
WESTERN DESIGN INSTITUTE, SAN FRANCISCO, CALIFORNIA

SHEET
5

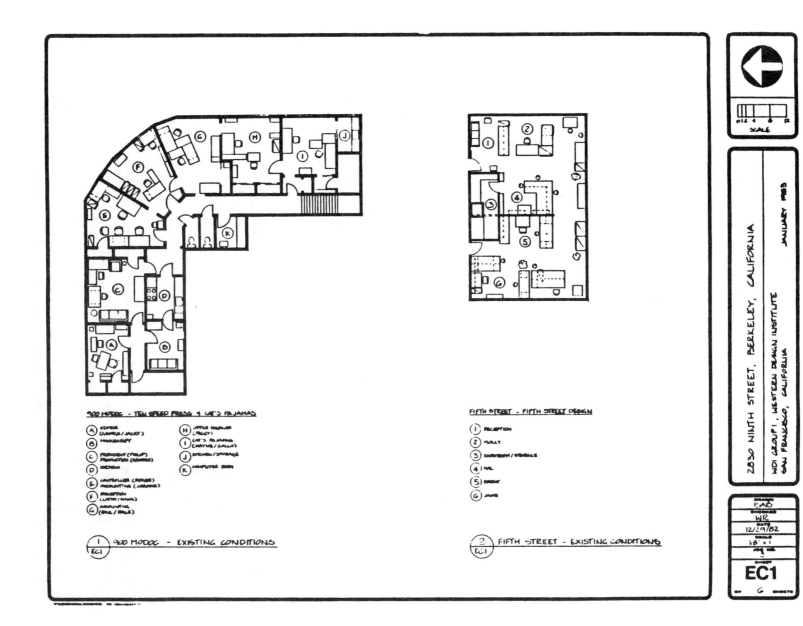

900 MODOC - TEN SPEED PRESS & CAT'S PAJAMAS

Ⓐ EDITOR (HOWARD / JACKIE)
Ⓑ HOUSEKEEPING
Ⓒ PRESIDENT (TONY) PRODUCTION (KONRAD)
Ⓓ KITCHEN
Ⓔ CONTROLLER (ROGER) ACCOUNTING (JEANINE)
Ⓕ RECEPTION (CATHY / MIMI)
Ⓖ ACCOUNTING (BILL / SALLY)

Ⓗ OFFICE MANAGER (PEGGY)
Ⓘ CAT'S PAJAMAS (KATHY / CALLA)
Ⓙ KITCHEN / STORAGE
Ⓚ COMPUTER ROOM

FIFTH STREET - FIFTH STREET DESIGN

① RECEPTION
② MOLLY
③ WORKROOM / STORAGE
④ HAL
⑤ BRENT
⑥ JANE

①/EC1 900 MODOC - EXISTING CONDITIONS

②/EC1 FIFTH STREET - EXISTING CONDITIONS

2830 NINTH STREET, BERKELEY, CALIFORNIA

HDI GROUP I, WESTERN DESIGN INSTITUTE
SAN FRANCISCO, CALIFORNIA

JANUARY 1983

DRAWN KAB
CHECKED WR
DATE 12/29/82
SCALE 1/8" = 1'
JOB NO.

EC1

OF 6 SHEETS

SCALE

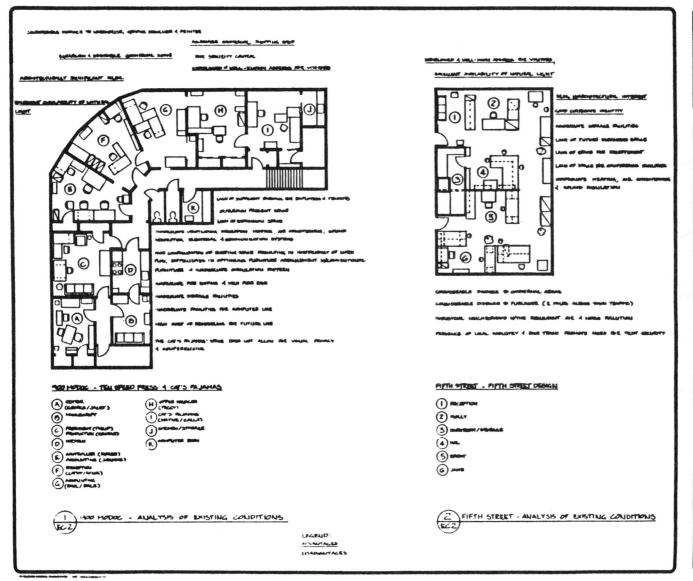

1 /EC2 900 MODOC - ANALYSIS OF EXISTING CONDITIONS

2 /EC2 FIFTH STREET - ANALYSIS OF EXISTING CONDITIONS

SCALE

2830 NINTH STREET, BERKELEY, CALIFORNIA

WDI GROUP 1, WESTERN DESIGN INSTITUTE
SAN FRANCISCO, CALIFORNIA

JANUARY 1983

EC2

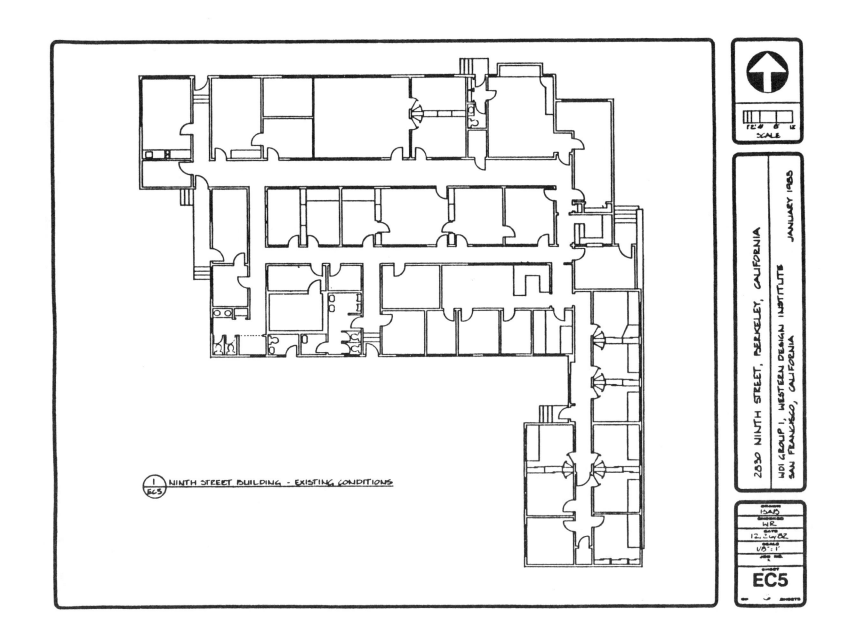

①/EC5 NINTH STREET BUILDING - EXISTING CONDITIONS

SCALE

2030 NINTH STREET, BERKELEY, CALIFORNIA

WDI GROUP I, WESTERN DESIGN INSTITUTE
SAN FRANCISCO, CALIFORNIA

JANUARY 1983

DRAWN
BAB
CHECKED
WR
DATE
12.24/82
SCALE
1/8" = 1'
JOB NO.
2

EC5

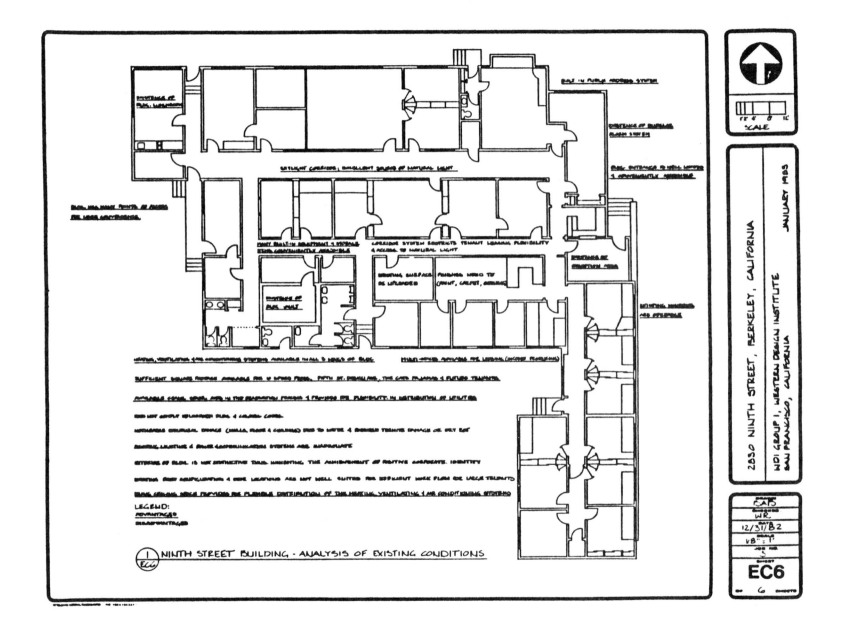

① NINTH STREET BUILDING - ANALYSIS OF EXISTING CONDITIONS

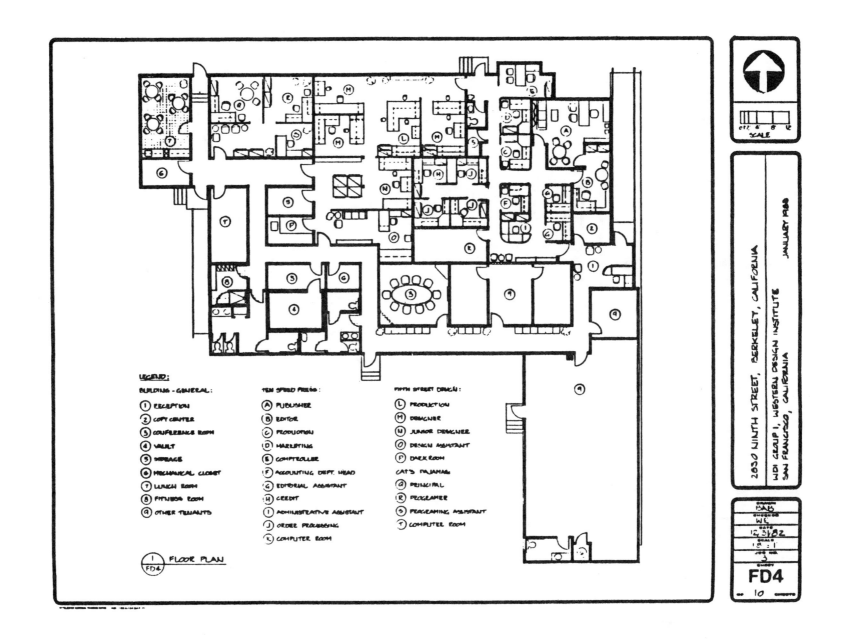

LEGEND:

BUILDING - GENERAL:
- (1) RECEPTION
- (2) COPY CENTER
- (3) CONFERENCE ROOM
- (4) VAULT
- (5) STORAGE
- (6) MECHANICAL CLOSET
- (7) LUNCH ROOM
- (8) FITNESS ROOM
- (9) OTHER TENANTS

TEN SPEED PRESS:
- (A) PUBLISHER
- (B) EDITOR
- (C) PRODUCTION
- (D) MARKETING
- (E) COMPTROLLER
- (F) ACCOUNTING DEPT. HEAD
- (G) EDITORIAL ASSISTANT
- (H) CREDIT
- (I) ADMINISTRATIVE ASSISTANT
- (J) ORDER PROCESSING
- (K) COMPUTER ROOM

FIFTH STREET DESIGN:
- (L) PRODUCTION
- (M) DESIGNER
- (N) JUNIOR DESIGNER
- (O) DESIGN ASSISTANT
- (P) DARK ROOM

CAT'S PAJAMAS:
- (Q) PRINCIPAL
- (R) PROGRAMER
- (S) PROGRAMING ASSISTANT
- (T) COMPUTER ROOM

(1 / FD4) FLOOR PLAN

2030 NINTH STREET, BERKELEY, CALIFORNIA

WDI GROUP 1, WESTERN DESIGN INSTITUTE
SAN FRANCISCO, CALIFORNIA

JANUARY 1988

SCALE

DRAWN	BAB
CHECKED	WC
DATE	12.31.82
SCALE	1/8 : 1
JOB NO.	3
SHEET	FD4
OF	10 SHEETS

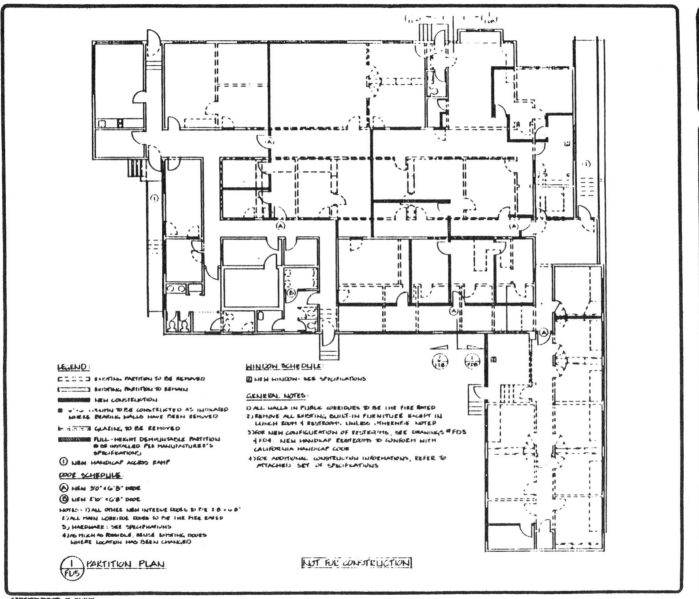

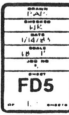

LEGEND:

EXISTING PARTITION TO BE REMOVED

EXISTING PARTITION TO REMAIN

NEW CONSTRUCTION

WALL COLUMN TO BE CONSTRUCTED AS INDICATED WHERE BEARING WALLS HAVE BEEN REMOVED

GLAZING TO BE REMOVED

FULL-HEIGHT DEMOUNTABLE PARTITION TO BE INSTALLED PER MANUFACTURER'S SPECIFICATIONS

① NEW HANDICAP ACCESS RAMP

DOOR SCHEDULE:

Ⓐ NEW 3'0" x 6'8" DOOR

Ⓑ NEW 2'10" x 6'8" DOOR

NOTES: 1) ALL OTHER NEW INTERIOR DOORS TO BE 2'8" x 6'8"
2) ALL MAIN CORRIDOR DOORS TO BE 1 HR FIRE RATED
3) HARDWARE: SEE SPECIFICATIONS
4) AS MUCH AS POSSIBLE, REUSE EXISTING DOORS WHERE LOCATION HAS BEEN CHANGED

WINDOW SCHEDULE:

Ⓦ NEW WINDOW: SEE SPECIFICATIONS

GENERAL NOTES:

1) ALL WALLS IN PUBLIC CORRIDORS TO BE 1 HR FIRE RATED
2) REMOVE ALL EXISTING BUILT-IN FURNITURE EXCEPT IN LUNCH ROOM & RESTROOM, UNLESS OTHERWISE NOTED
3) FOR NEW CONFIGURATION OF RESTROOMS, SEE DRAWINGS # FD3 & FD4. NEW HANDICAP RESTROOMS TO CONFORM WITH CALIFORNIA HANDICAP CODE
4) FOR ADDITIONAL CONSTRUCTION INFORMATION, REFER TO ATTACHED SET OF SPECIFICATIONS

⬚¹/FD5 PARTITION PLAN

[NOT FOR CONSTRUCTION]

2820 NINTH STREET, BERKELEY, CALIFORNIA

WDI GROUP   WESTERN DESIGN INSTITUTE
SAN FRANCISCO   CALIFORNIA

JANUARY '83

DRAWN	P. AF.
CHECKED	W.K.
DATE	1/14/83
SCALE	1/8" = 1'
JOB NO	

SHEET

FD5

OF   1   SHEETS

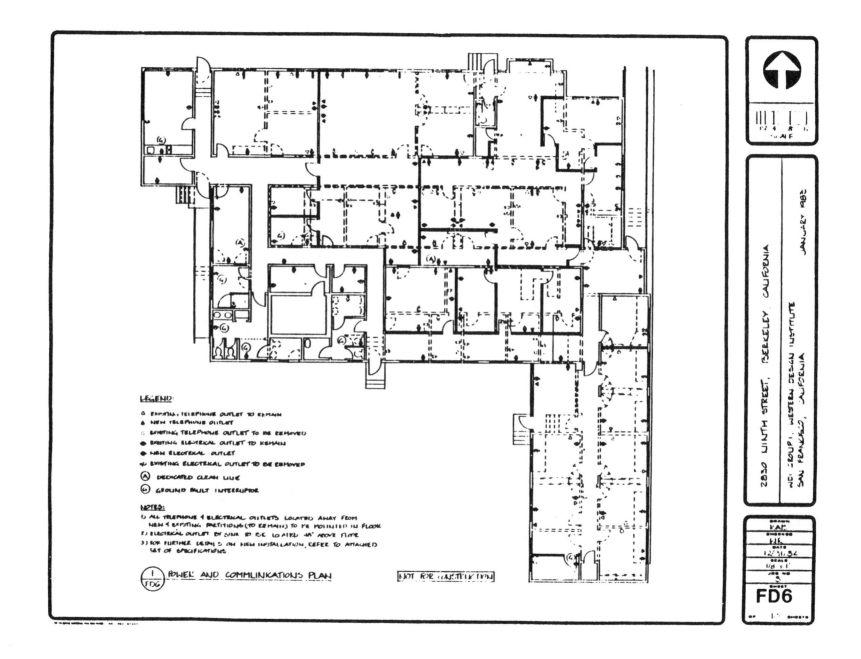

LEGEND:

◦ EXISTING TELEPHONE OUTLET TO REMAIN
▲ NEW TELEPHONE OUTLET
∴ EXISTING TELEPHONE OUTLET TO BE REMOVED
● EXISTING ELECTRICAL OUTLET TO REMAIN
● NEW ELECTRICAL OUTLET
⊬ EXISTING ELECTRICAL OUTLET TO BE REMOVED
Ⓐ DEDICATED CLEAN LINE
Ⓖ GROUND FAULT INTERRUPTER

NOTES:
1) ALL TELEPHONE & ELECTRICAL OUTLETS LOCATED AWAY FROM
   NEW & EXISTING PARTITIONS (TO REMAIN) TO BE MOUNTED IN FLOOR
2) ELECTRICAL OUTLET BY SINK TO BE LOCATED 44" ABOVE FLOOR
3) FOR FURTHER DETAILS ON NEW INSTALLATION, REFER TO ATTACHED
   SET OF SPECIFICATIONS

(1/FD6) POWER AND COMMUNICATIONS PLAN

NOT FOR CONSTRUCTION

2830 NINTH STREET, BERKELEY, CALIFORNIA

WD GROUP, WESTERN DESIGN INSTITUTE
SAN FRANCISCO, CALIFORNIA

JANUARY 1983

DRAWN
KAF
CHECKED
HR
DATE
12/31/82
SCALE
1/8"=1'
JOB NO
5
SHEET
FD6
OF 15 SHEETS

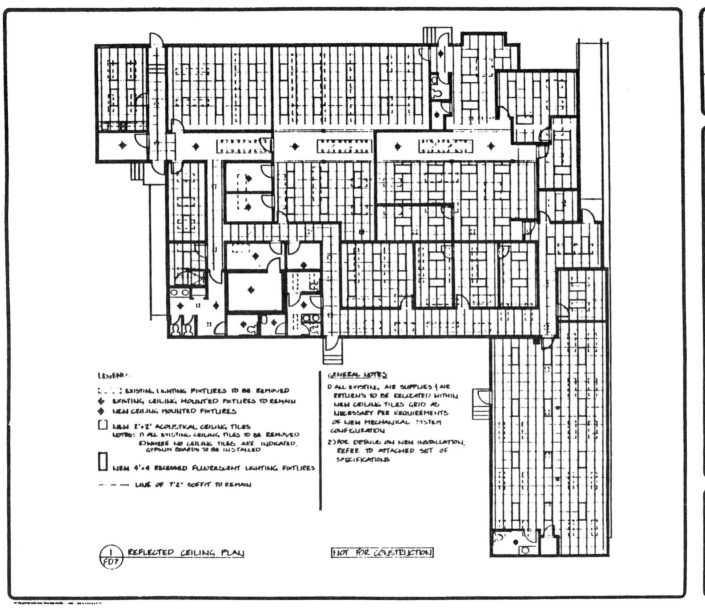

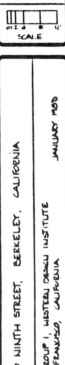

2830 NINTH STREET, BERKELEY, CALIFORNIA

HDR GROUP 1, WESTERN DESIGN INSTITUTE
SAN FRANCISCO, CALIFORNIA

JANUARY 1985

SCALE

DRAWN BAS
CHECKED WR
DATE 1.10.85
SCALE 1/8" = 1'
JOB NO 3
SHEET
FD7
OF 10 SHEETS

LEGEND:

⬚ EXISTING LIGHTING FIXTURES TO BE REMOVED
◆ EXISTING CEILING MOUNTED FIXTURES TO REMAIN
◆ NEW CEILING MOUNTED FIXTURES

☐ NEW 2'×2' ACOUSTICAL CEILING TILES
NOTE: 1) ALL EXISTING CEILING TILES TO BE REMOVED
2) WHERE NO CEILING TILES ARE INDICATED,
GYPSUM BOARDS TO BE INSTALLED

☐ NEW 4'×4' RECESSED FLUORESCENT LIGHTING FIXTURES

– – – LINE OF 7'2" SOFFIT TO REMAIN

GENERAL NOTES:

1) ALL EXISTING AIR SUPPLIES & AIR
RETURNS TO BE RELOCATED WITHIN
NEW CEILING TILES GRID AS
NECESSARY PER REQUIREMENTS
OF NEW MECHANICAL SYSTEM
CONFIGURATION

2) FOR DETAILS ON NEW INSTALLATION,
REFER TO ATTACHED SET OF
SPECIFICATIONS

(1/FD7) REFLECTED CEILING PLAN

NOT FOR CONSTRUCTION

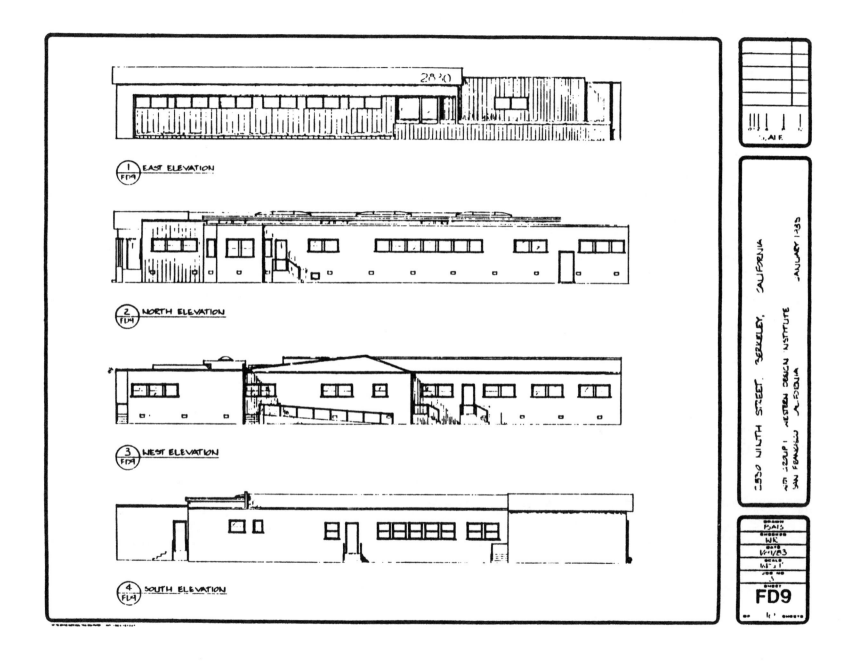

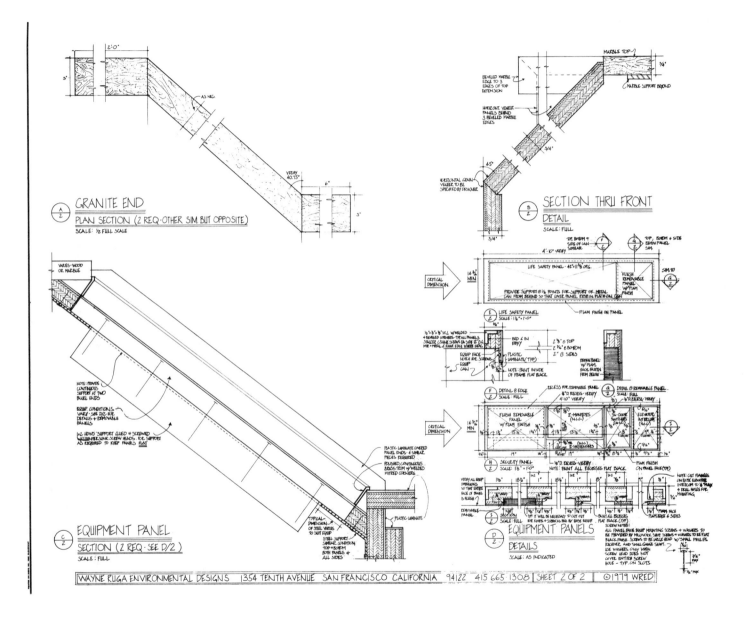

GRANITE END
PLAN SECTION (2 REQ·OTHER SIM. BUT OPPOSITE)
SCALE: ½ FULL SCALE

SECTION THRU FRONT
DETAIL
SCALE: FULL

EQUIPMENT PANEL
SECTION (2 REQ·SEE D/2)
SCALE: FULL

EQUIPMENT PANELS
DETAILS
SCALE: AS INDICATED

LIFE SAFETY PANEL
SCALE: 1⅛"·1'-0"

SECURITY PANEL
SCALE: 1⅛"·1'-0"

WAYNE RUGA ENVIRONMENTAL DESIGNS   1354 TENTH AVENUE   SAN FRANCISCO CALIFORNIA   94122   415 665 1308 | SHEET 2 OF 2 | ©1979 WRED

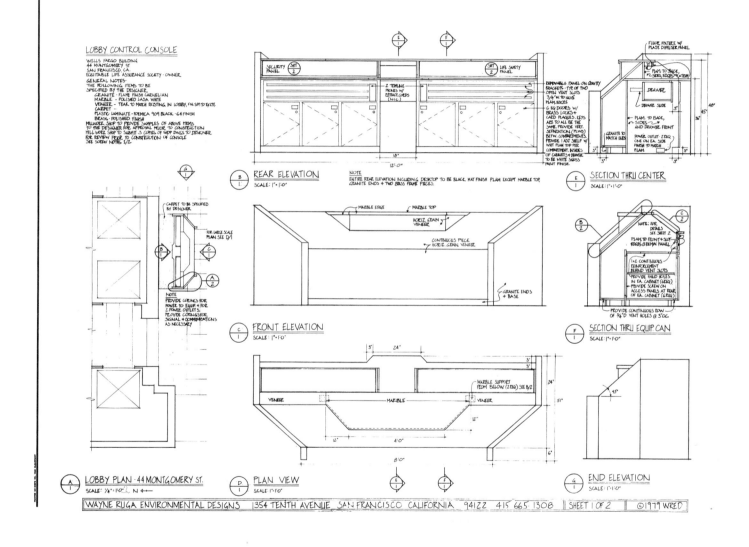

LOBBY CONTROL CONSOLE

WELLS FARGO BUILDING
44 MONTGOMERY ST
SAN FRANCISCO, CA.
EQUITABLE LIFE ASSURANCE SOCIETY · OWNER
GENERAL NOTES:
THE FOLLOWING ITEMS TO BE
SPECIFIED BY THE DESIGNER
   GRANITE - FLAME FINISH CARNELIAN
   MARBLE - POLISHED LASA WHITE
   VENEER - TEAK TO MATCH EXISTING IN LOBBY, FIN SIM TO EXIST.
   CARPET -
   PLASTIC LAMINATE - FORMICA 909 BLACK · 64 FINISH
   BRASS · POLISHED FINISH
MILLWORK SHOP TO PROVIDE SAMPLES OF ABOVE ITEMS
TO THE DESIGNER FOR APPROVAL PRIOR TO CONSTRUCTION
MILLWORK SHOP TO SUBMIT 3 COPIES OF SHOP DWGS TO DESIGNER
FOR REVIEW PRIOR TO CONSTRUCTION OF CONSOLE
SEE SCREW NOTES 1/2

REAR ELEVATION
SCALE: 1"=1'-0"

NOTE
ENTIRE REAR ELEVATION INCLUDING DESKTOP TO BE BLACK, MAT FINISH PLAM EXCEPT MARBLE TOP,
GRANITE ENDS & TWO BRASS FRAME PIECES.

SECTION THRU CENTER
SCALE: 1"=1'-0"

FRONT ELEVATION
SCALE: 1"=1'-0"

SECTION THRU EQUIP CAN
SCALE: 1"=1'-0"

LOBBY PLAN · 44 MONTGOMERY ST.
SCALE: 1/4"=1'-0" N

PLAN VIEW
SCALE: 1"=1'-0"

END ELEVATION
SCALE: 1"=1'-0"

WAYNE RUGA ENVIRONMENTAL DESIGNS 1354 TENTH AVENUE SAN FRANCISCO CALIFORNIA 94122 415 665 1308 ║ SHEET 1 OF 2 ║ ©1979 WRED

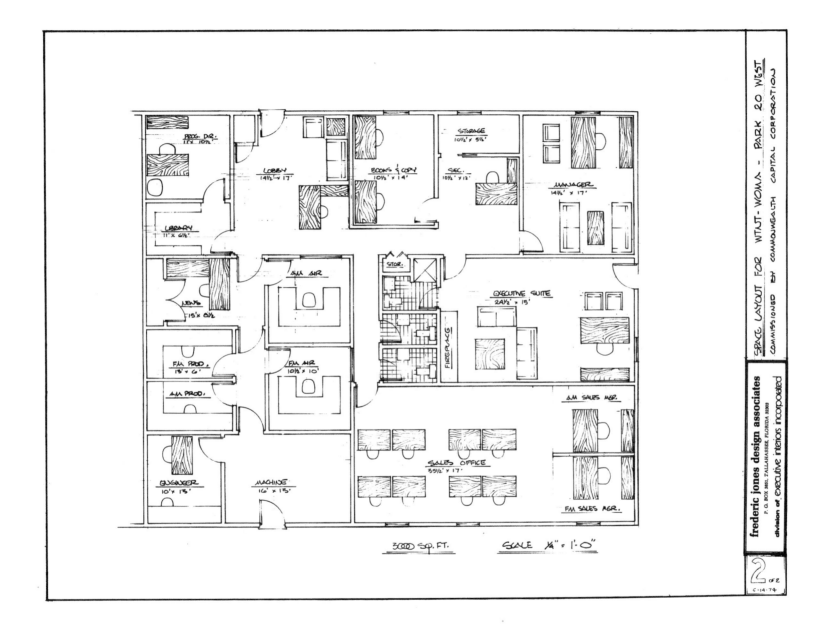

SPACE LAYOUT FOR WTJT-WOMA - PARK 20 WEST
COMMISSIONED BY COMMONWEALTH CAPITAL CORPORATION

frederic jones design associates
P. O. BOX 3851, TALLAHASSEE, FLORIDA 32303
division of executive interiors incorporated

2 OF 2
5-14-74

3000 SQ. FT.   SCALE ⅛" = 1'-0"

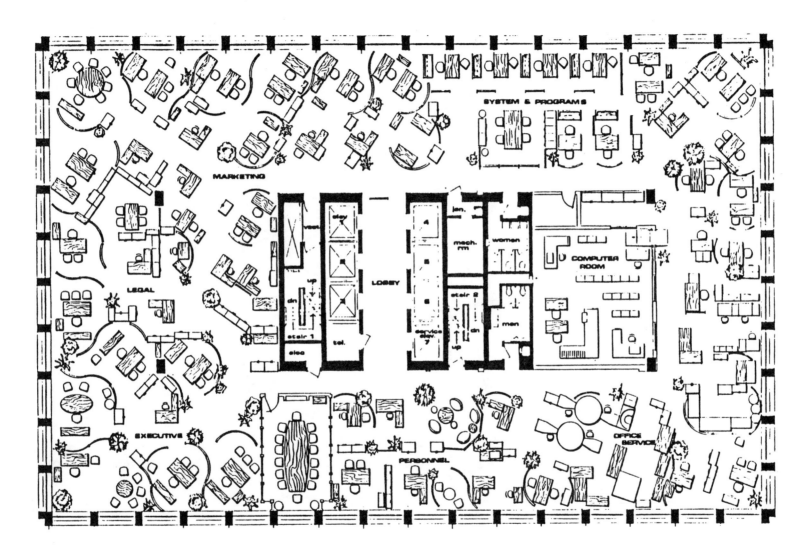

21ST FLOOR

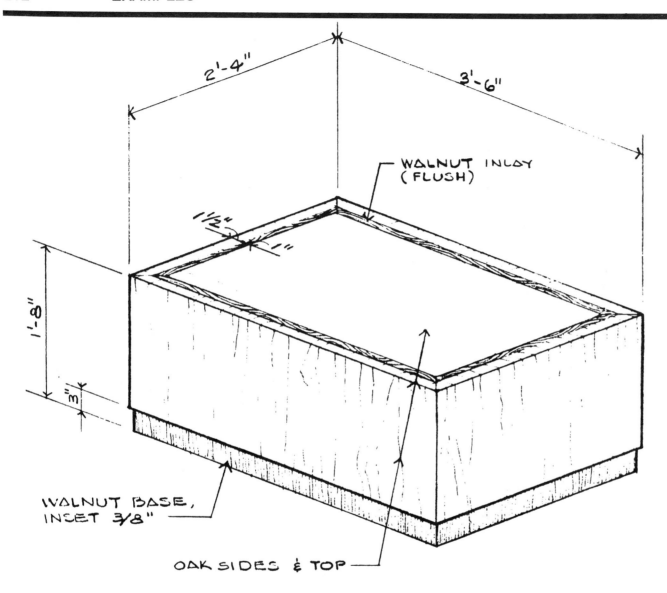

2'-4"

3'-6"

WALNUT INLAY
(FLUSH)

1½"

1"

1'-8"

3"

WALNUT BASE,
INSET ⅜"

OAK SIDES & TOP

NOTE:
DETAILS & FINISH
SHALL MATCH COFFEE
TABLE IN SAME
LOCATION.

END TABLE

RECEPTION AREA, 31ST. FLOOR

ISOMETRIC DRAWING
SCALE: 1"=1'-0"   RMK

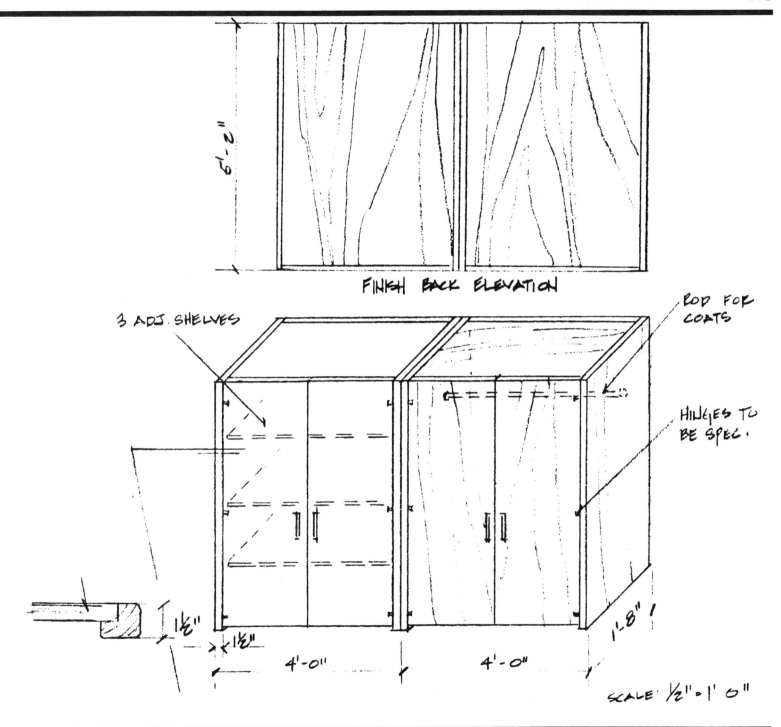

FINISH BACK ELEVATION

3 ADJ. SHELVES

ROD FOR COATS

HINGES TO BE SPEC.

6'-2"

1½"

1½"

1½"

4'-0"

4'-0"

1'-8"

SCALE: ½" = 1' 0"

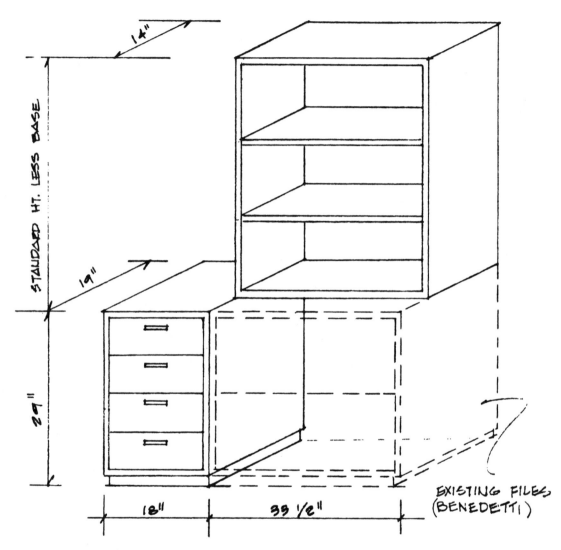

STANDARD HT. LESS BASE

14"

19"

29"

18"

39 1/2"

EXISTING FILES
(BENEDETTI)

ISOMETRIC DRAWING
SCALE : 1/16 = 1'-0"

NEW BOX DRAWER CABINET
AND BOOK CASE
WALNUT · OIL FINISH
DRAWERS. FULL EXTENSION

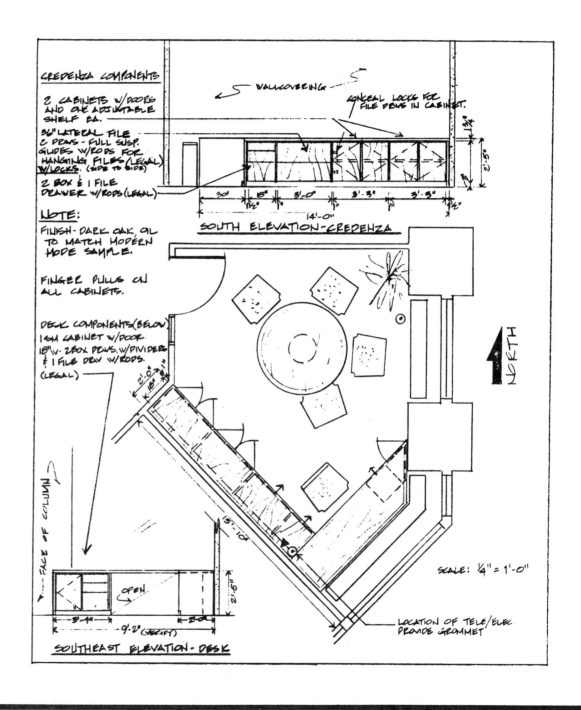

CREDENZA COMPONENTS

2 CABINETS W/DOORS AND ONE ADJUSTABLE SHELF EA.

36" LATERAL FILE 2 DRWS - FULL SUSP. GLIDES W/RODS FOR HANGING FILES (LEGAL) W/LOCKS. (SIDE TO SIDE)

2 BOX & 1 FILE DRAWER W/RODS (LEGAL)

NOTE:
FINISH- DARK OAK, OIL TO MATCH MODERN MODE SAMPLE.

FINGER PULLS ON ALL CABINETS.

DESK COMPONENTS (BELOW)
1 SM CABINET W/DOOR.
18" W- 2 BOX DRWS. W/DIVIDER & 1 FILE DRW W/RODS.
(LEGAL)

WALLCOVERING

CONCEAL LOCKS FOR FILE DRWS IN CABINET.

SOUTH ELEVATION - CREDENZA

14'-0"

NORTH

SCALE: 1/4" = 1'-0"

LOCATION OF TELE/ELEC PROVIDE GROMMET

FACE OF COLUMN

OPEN

SOUTHEAST ELEVATION - DESK

9'-2" (VERIFY)

EXISTING CREDENZAS (TO BE MODIFIED):

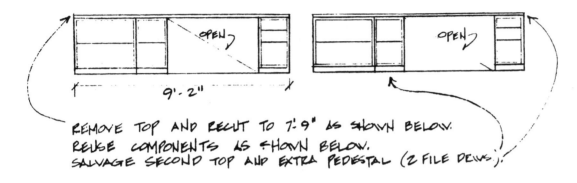

9'-2"

REMOVE TOP AND RECUT TO 7'-9" AS SHOWN BELOW.
REUSE COMPONENTS AS SHOWN BELOW.
SALVAGE SECOND TOP AND EXTRA PEDESTAL (2 FILE DWS.)

NEW CONFIGURATION:

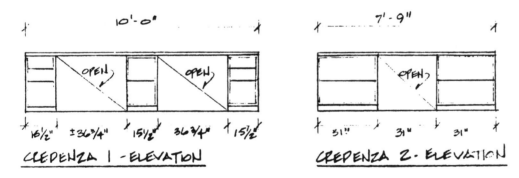

10'-0"   7'-9"

15½" ±36¾" 15½" 36¾" 15½"   31"   31"   31"

CREDENZA 1 - ELEVATION   CREDENZA 2 - ELEVATION

CR-1 - NEW TOP - 10'-0"L. × 24" D. - PLASTIC LAMINATE TO MATCH EXIST'G.
         REUSE EXIST'G WALNUT PEDESTALS (15½"W.) AS SHOWN.
         ATTACH NEW TOP - LEAVE KNEESPACE AS SHOWN.

CR-2 - RECUT EXIST'G TOP (9'-2") TO 7'-9" × 18" D.
         ATTACH TO EXIST'G WALNUT LATERAL FILES AS SHOWN.

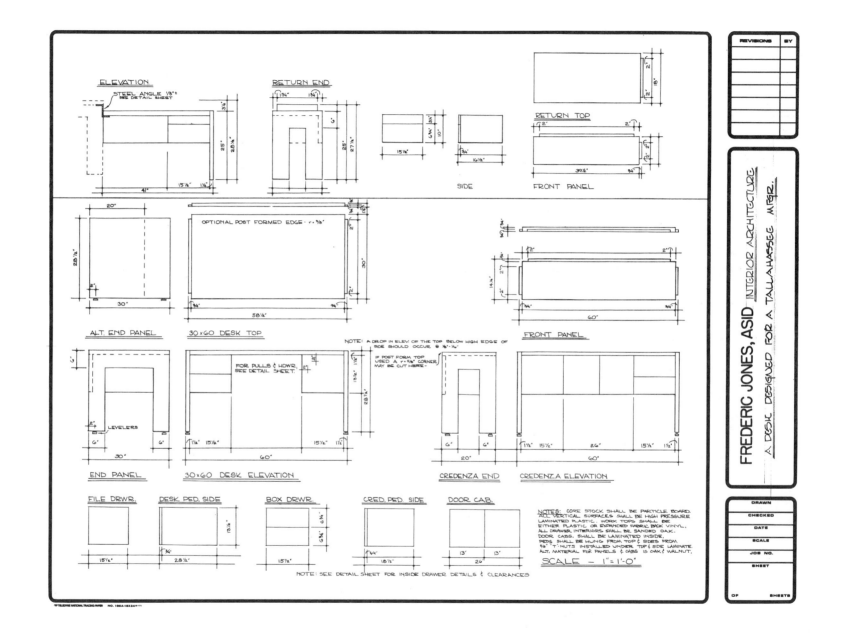

ELEVATION

RETURN END

RETURN TOP

SIDE   FRONT PANEL

ALT. END PANEL   30 x 60 DESK TOP

OPTIONAL POST FORMED EDGE · r · ⅜"

FRONT PANEL

NOTE: A DROP IN ELEV. OF THE TOP BELOW HIGH EDGE OF SIDE SHOULD OCCUR @ ⅜"-½"

END PANEL   30 x 60 DESK ELEVATION

FOR PULLS & HDWR, SEE DETAIL SHEET.

IF POST FORM TOP USED A · r · ⅝" CORNER MAY BE CUT HERE

CREDENZA END   CREDENZA ELEVATION

FILE DRWR.   DESK PED. SIDE   BOX DRWR.   CRED. PED SIDE   DOOR CAB.

LEVELERS

STEEL ANGLE ⅛" ± SEE DETAIL SHEET

NOTES: CORE STOCK SHALL BE PARTICLE BOARD. ALL VERTICAL SURFACES SHALL BE HIGH PRESSURE LAMINATED PLASTIC. WORK TOPS SHALL BE EITHER PLASTIC OR EXPANDED FABRIC BACK VINYL. ALL DRAWER INTERIORS SHALL BE SANDED OAK. DOOR CABS. SHALL BE LAMINATED INSIDE. PEDS. SHALL BE HUNG FROM TOP & SIDES FROM ⅝" T-NUTS INSTALLED UNDER TOP & SIDE LAMINATE. ALT. MATERIAL FOR PANELS & CABS IS OAK & WALNUT.

SCALE – 1" = 1'-0"

NOTE: SEE DETAIL SHEET FOR INSIDE DRAWER DETAILS & CLEARANCES

FREDERIC JONES, ASID INTERIOR ARCHITECTURE

A DESK DESIGNED FOR A TALLAHASSEE MFGR.

REVISIONS | BY

DRAWN
CHECKED
DATE
SCALE
JOB NO.
SHEET

OF   SHEETS

FINISH SCHEDULE — JONES & FELDMAN DESIGN ASSOCIATES: ROCKRIDGE ALBANY

ROCKRIDGE HEALTH CARE PLAN, INC.
1500 16th STREET, SAN FRANCISCO, CA. 94103

DRAWN: G.F.
DATE: 10-5-82
SCALE: N.T.S.
SHEET 5 OF 5 SHEETS

RM NO.	ROOM DESIGNATION	FLOOR	BASE	NORTH MATL	FIN	(x)	EAST MATL	FIN	(x)	SOUTH MATL	FIN	(x)	WEST MATL	FIN	(x)	CLG/SOFFIT MATL	FIN	HT	REMARKS
101	EXAMINATION	E	5	6	X	④	6	X	①	6	X	①	6	X	④				DR WALL ②
102	EXAMINATION	E	5	6	X	①	6	X	D.O.	6	Y	D.O.	6	X	①				DR WALL ②
103	EXAMINATION	E	5	6	X	D.O.	6	Y	D.O.	6	Y	D.O.	6	X	D.O.				
104	EXAMINATION	E	5	6	X	D.O.	6	X	⑤	6	X	D.O.	6	X	D.O.				
105	MENS TOILET	G	F	M	Y	D.O.	M	Z	⑤	M	Y	D.O.	M	Y	⑤				
106	WOMENS TOILET	G	F	M	Y	D.O.	M	Y	D.O.	M	Y	D.O.	M	Z	⑥				
107	OFFICE	C	5	11	X	①	11	X	D.O.	11	X	D.O.	11	X	①				
108	PHARMACY	D	5	6	X	D.O.	6	X	D.O.	6	X	D.O.	6	X	D.O.				
109	PHARMACY STORAGE	D	5	5	X	④	6	X	⑥A	6	X	D.O.	6	X	D.O.				
110	OPTOMETRY/WORK	D	5	6	X	①	6	X	①	6	X	D.O.	6	X	⑥				
111	OPTOMETRY/EXAMINATION	E	5	6	X	④	6	X	D.O.	7	X	D.O.							
112	OPTOMETRY OFFICE	B	5	11	Y	D.O.	11	X	④	11	X	D.O.	11	X	①				
113	OPTOMETRY/WORK RM.	B	5	11	X	①	11	X	2-4⑥	11	X	2-4⑥	11	Y	—				
114	OPTOMETRY/FITTING	B	5.	11	X	2-4⑥	11	X	2-4⑥	11	X	①	6	X	D.O.				
115	OPTOMETRY/WAITING	B	5	11	XY	①	11	XY	D.O.	11	XY	④	11	XY	⑤				
116	LOBBY	A	5	11	XY	2-4⑥	11	XY	—	11	XY	⑥m	11	XY	①				
117	CONSULTATION	B	5	11	XY	①	11	XY	②	11	XY	⑥	11	XY	④				
118	EXAMINATION	E	5	6	X	D.O.	6	X	①	6	X	D.O.	6	X	②				
119	EXAMINATION	E	5	6	X	D.O.	6	X	D.O.	6	X	D.O.	6	X	①				
120	CONSULTATION	B	5	11	X	D.O.	11	X	⑤	6	X	①	11	X	D.O.				
121	URIN. TOILET	G	F	Y	M	②	Y	M	①	Y	M	①	Y	M	2-4⑥				
122	TOILET	G	F	Y	M	D.O.	Y	M	①	Y	M	D.O.	Y	M	2-4⑥				
123	DRAW STATION	D	5	6	X	①	6	X	D.O.	6	X	D.O.	6	X	①				
124	INTERVIEW	D	5	11	XY	D.O.	11	XY	—	11	XY	D.O.	N	Y	D.O.				
125	LAB/WORK AREA	D	5	6	X	D.O.	6	X	D.O.	6	X	—	6	X	?				
126	NURSE STATION	B	5	11	XY	D.O.	11	XY	—	11	XY	①	N	Y	①				
127	SICK CHILD/WAITING	A	5	11	XY	—	2	XY	①	11	XY	—	0	Y	①				PAINT THE ELEVATOR DOOR 11
128	INTERVIEW	B	5	11	XY	①	11	XY	D.O.	11	XY	①	N	Y	①				
129	CENTRAL WAIT.	A	5	11	XY	D.O.	11	XY	D.O.	11	X	D.O.	11	XY	D.O.				
130	ADMITTING	H	5	J	XY	D.O.	11	XY	D.O.	11	XY	D.O.	11	XY	D.O.				
131	STERILIZATION	D	5	6	X	D.O.	5	X	D.O.	6	X	④	6	X	④				DOOR/FRAME ②
132	SOILED HOLDING	D	5	5	X	②	5	X	D.O.	5	X	①	5	X	①				
133	CONSULTATION	B	5	11	X	D.O.	11	X	②	11	X	2-4⑥	11	X	D.O.				
134	EXAMINATION	E	5	6	X	①	6	X	①	6	X	D.O.	6	X	②				
135	EXAMINATION	E	5	6	X	D.O.	6	X	D.O.	6	X	D.O.	6	X	①				
136	CONSULTATION	B	5	11	X	D.O.	11	X	③	11	X	①	11	X	D.O.				
137	EXAMINATION	E	5	6	X	D.O.	6	X	④	6	X	④	6	X	D.O.				DR WALL ②
138	EXAMINATION	E	5	6	X	D.O.	6	X	④	6	X	④	6	X	D.O.				DR WALL ②
139	EXAMINATION	E	5	6	X	D.O.	6	X	①	6	X	①	6	X	③				
140	EXAMINATION	E	5	11	XY	②	11	XY	①	11	X	④	11	XY	③				
141	ADMINISTRATION	C	5	11	X	—	11	X	D.O.	11	X	—	11	X	D.O.				
142	MEDICAL RECORDS	C	5	11	X	—	11	X	D.O.	11	X	④	5	X	⑤				
143	OFFICE	C	5	11	X	②	11	X	—	11	X	①	11	X	—				
144	OFFICE	C	5	11	X	—	11	X	①	11	X	④	11	X	⑤				2×6 STUDS & STAIR
145	OFFICE	C	5	11	X	①	11	X	④	11	X	D.O.	11	X	①				DOOR ①
146	STAIRS	C	5	11	XY	②	11	XY	①	11	X	④	11	XY	③				
147	COPY/COM.	B	5	11	XY	D.O.	11	XY	—	11	XY	D.O.	11	XY	—				
148	JANITOR	D	5			①						④							
149	not used																		
150	REFUGE	D	5			D.X.			①			①			?				1st finish
151	STORAGE	D	5			D.X.			D.X.			D.X.			?				
152	STORAGE	D	5			D.X.			D.X.			D.X.			?				
153	ELECTRICAL EQUIPMENT																	?	
154	MEETING	C	5	11	X	④	11	X	②	11	X	①	11	X	?				PAINTED STRIPE EAST/NORTH/WEST
155	not used	C	5	5	X		5	X		5	X		5	X					
156	not used																		
157	LOCKERS					④			①			①			④				
158	PLAYROOM					D.O.			②			②							

RM NO.	ROOM DESIGNATION	FLOOR	BASE	NORTH MATL	FIN	(x)	EAST MATL	FIN	(x)	SOUTH MATL	FIN	(x)	WEST MATL	FIN	(x)	CLG/SOFFIT MATL	FIN	HT	REMARKS
159	RADIOLOGY	D	5	6	X	⑩	5	X	④	6	X	⑥	6	X	⑥				
160	VIEWING	D	5	6	X	⑥	6	X	①	6	X	②	6	X	②				
161	DARK ROOM	D	5	6	X	D.O.	6	X	④	6	X	D.O.	6	X	①				
162	WAITING	B	5	11	XY	①	11	XY	①	11	XY	④	11	XY	②				
163	OFFICE	C	5	11	X	②	11	X	⑦	11	X	①	11	X	—				
164	NURSES STATION	C	5	11	X	—	11	X	—	11	X	④	11	Y	D.O.				
165	OFFICE	C	5	11	X	D.O.	11	X	①	11	X	④	11	X	④				
166	OFFICE	C	5	11	X	④	11	X	①	11	X	④	11	X	D.O.				
167	OFFICE	C	5	11	X	①	11	X	D.O.	11	X	⑦	11	X	D.O.				
168	TREATMENT	D	5	6	X	④	6	X	④	6	X	④	6	X	②				
169	not used																		
170	CAST ROOM	D	5	6	X	②	6	X	①	6	X	④	6	X	D.O.				
171	TOILET	G	F	Y	M	D.O.	Y	M	D.O.	Y	M	①	Y	M	①				
172	AUDIO	D	5	6	X	D.O.	6	X	④	6	X	④	6	X	D.O.				
173	STAIRS	C	5	11	XY	—	11	XY	②	11	XY	②	11	XY	④				
201	BUSINESS OFFICE	C	5	11	X		11	X		11	X		11	X					
202	COMPUTER RM.	C	5	11	X		11	X		11	X		11	X					
203	OFFICE	C	5	11	X		11	X		11	X		11	X					
204	OFFICE	C	5	11	X		11	X		11	X		11	X					
205	CONFERENCE RM.	A	5	Y	P		Y	P		Y	P		Y	P					
206	OFFICE	B	5	11	X		11	X		11	X		11	X					
207	"	B	5	11	X		11	X		11	X		11	X					
208	"	B	5	11	Q		11	X		11	X		11	X					
209	"	B	5	11	X		11	X		11	X		11	X					
210	"	B	5	11	X		11	X		11	X		11	X					
211	STAIR	C	5	11	XY		11	XY		11	XY		11	XY					
212	OFFICE	B	5	11	Y		11	Y		11	Y		11	Y					
213	"	B	5	11	X		11	X		Y	K		11	X					
214	"	C	5	11	X		11	X		11	X		11	X					
215	MARKETING	C	5	11	X		11	X		11	X		11	X					
216	WORK RM.	C	5	11	X		11	X		11	X		11	X					
217	OFFICE	C	5	11	X		11	X		11	Y		11	X					
218	OFFICE	C	5	3	X		3	X		3	X		3	X					
219	STORAGE	D	5	6	X		6	X		6	X		6	X					
220	WOMEN	G	F	Y	M		Y	M		Z	F		Y	M					
221	MEN	G	F	Z	F		Y	F		Y	M		Y	M					
222	STAIR	C	5	11	XY		11	XY		11	XY		11	XY					
223	JANITOR	D	5	6	X		6	X		6	X		6	X					
224	STAFF LOUNGE	D	5	5	X		5	X		6	X		6	X					
225	ELEVATOR	A	5	B	B		B	B		B	B		B	B					CARPET WALLS
226	EQUIP. RM.	D	5	6	X		6	X		6	X		6	X					
227	OFFICE	C	5	11	X		11	X		11	X		11	X					
228	"	C	5	11	X		11	X		11	X		11	X					
229	WAITING	C	5	2	5		2	5		2	5		2	5					
230	SHOWER	G	F	F	Z		F	Z		F	Z		F	Z					

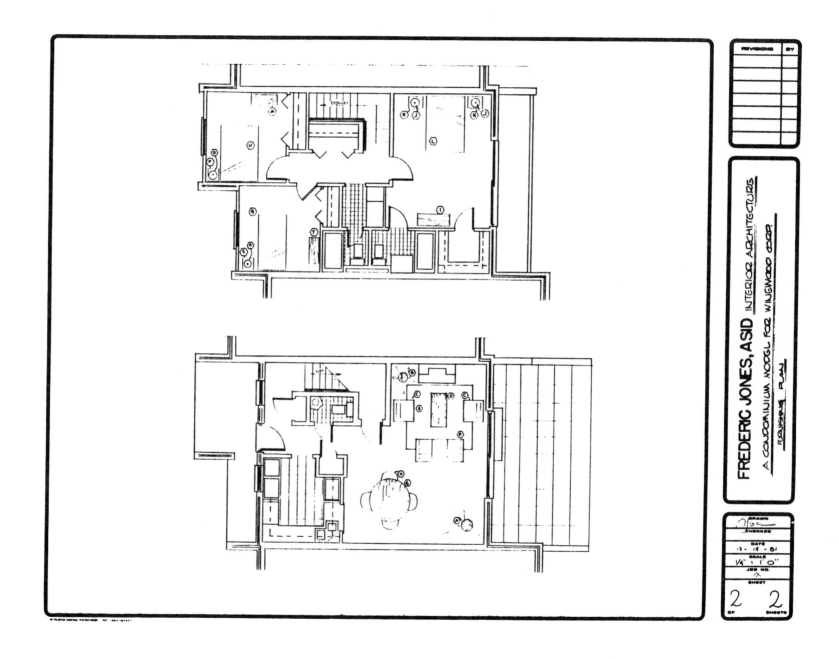

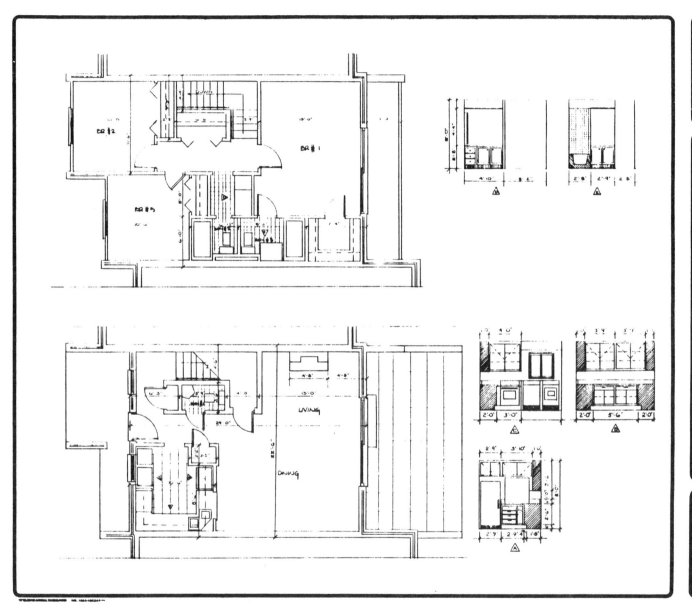

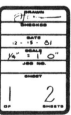

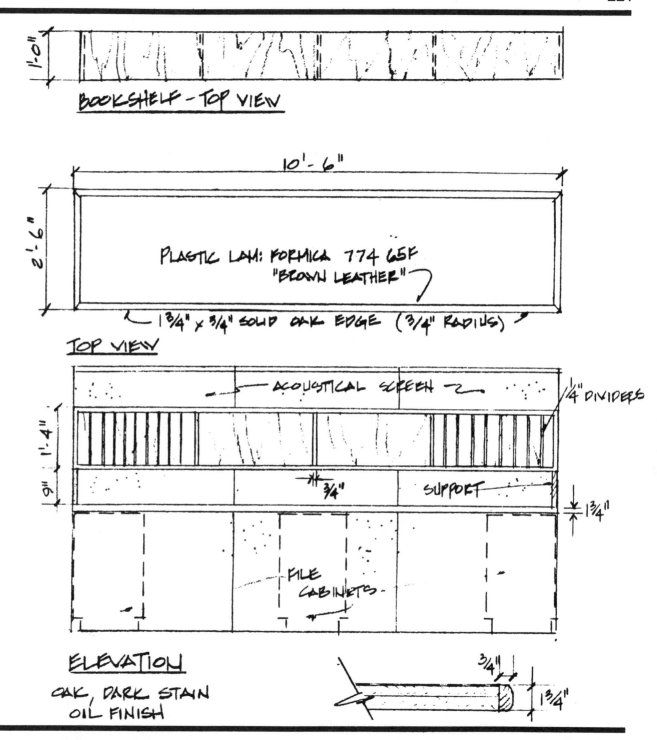

1'-0"

BOOKSHELF - TOP VIEW

10'-6"

2'-6"

PLASTIC LAM: FORMICA 774 65F
"BROWN LEATHER"

1³/₄" x ³/₄" SOLID OAK EDGE (³/₄" RADIUS)

TOP VIEW

ACOUSTICAL SCREEN

¼" DIVIDERS

1'-4"

9"

³/₄"

SUPPORT

1³/₄"

FILE CABINETS

ELEVATION

OAK, DARK STAIN
OIL FINISH

³/₄"

1³/₄"

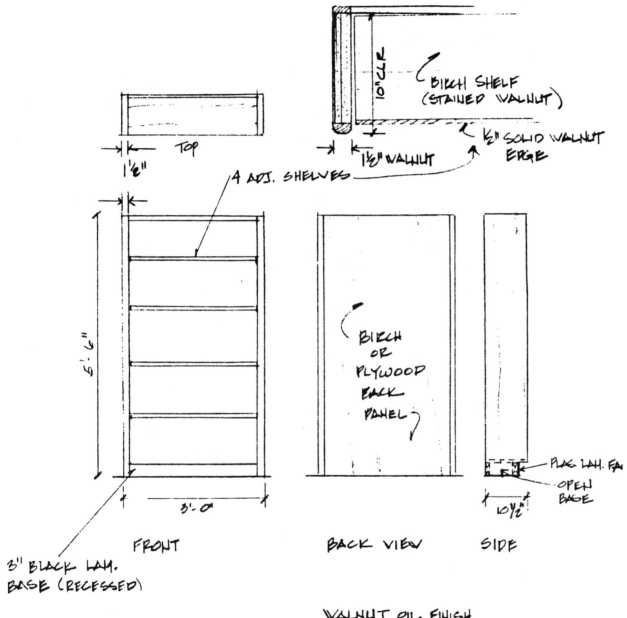

TOP

1½"

BIRCH SHELF
(STAINED WALNUT)

10" CLR

1½" WALNUT

½" SOLID WALNUT
EDGE

4 ADJ. SHELVES

5'-6"

BIRCH
OR
PLYWOOD
BACK
PANEL

3'-0"

10½"

PLAS. LAM. FA.

OPEN
BASE

FRONT   BACK VIEW   SIDE

3" BLACK LAM.
BASE (RECESSED)

WALNUT, OIL FINISH

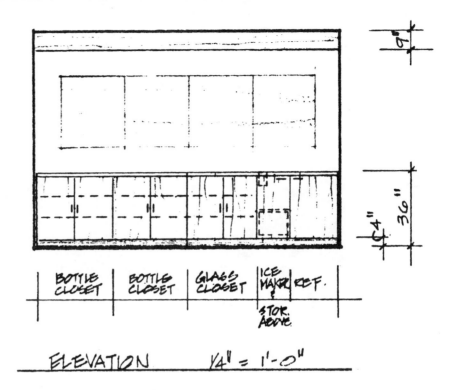

BOTTLE CLOSET	BOTTLE CLOSET	GLASS CLOSET	ICE MAKER	REF.

STOR. ABOVE.

9"

36"

4"

ELEVATION   ¼" = 1'-0"

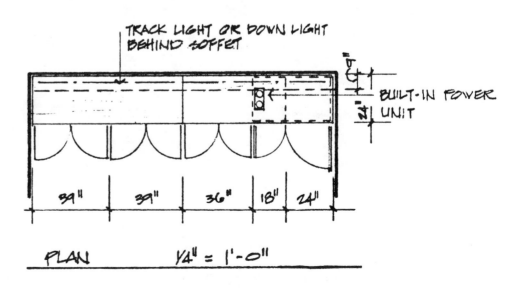

TRACK LIGHT OR DOWN LIGHT BEHIND SOFFET

BUILT-IN POWER UNIT

9"

24"

39"	39"	36"	18"	24"

PLAN   ¼" = 1'-0"

RENDERER: Helmut Jacoby
ARCHITECTS: Hellmuth, Obata and Kassabaum Inc.

McDonnell Planetarium, St. Louis, Mo. 1959

Giovanni Battista Piranesi

Interior of S. Constanza in Rome (A.D. 330)
from Antichita Romane or circ. 1748-1791

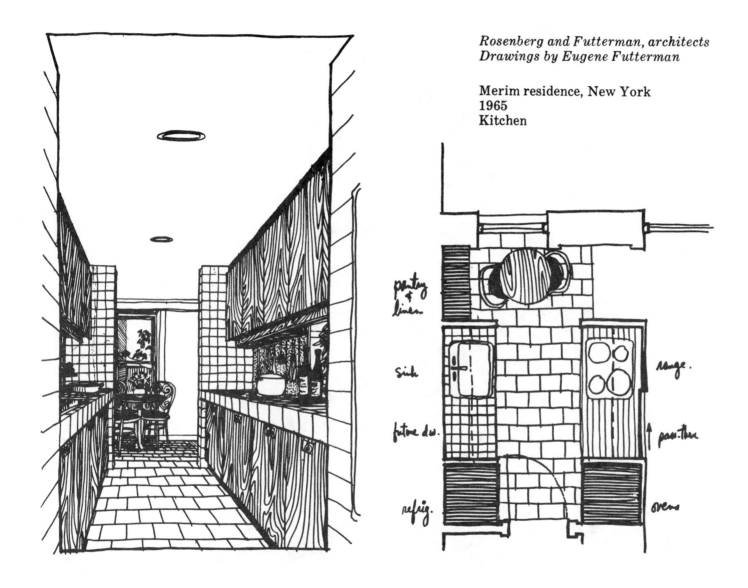

Rosenberg and Futterman, architects
Drawings by Eugene Futterman

Merim residence, New York
1965
Kitchen

RENDERER: Eugene Futterman
ARCHITECTS: Rosenberg and Futterman

Merim Residence, Kitchen, New York 1965

ARCHITECT: Paul Roudolph

Chapel for Tuskegee Institute, Tuskegee, Al.

RENDERER: Elizabeth Tanna
DESIGNER: R.M.K. Design

Arthur Young Accounting Offices, San Francisco

EXTENDED SOCIAL QUARTER
NEUTRA & ALEXANDER
INT.2   ARCHITECTS

EXTENDED SOCIAL QARTERS
NEUTRA & ALEXANDER
INT.1   ARCHITECTS

ARCHITECTS: Neutra and Alexander

Housing Project in Montana

RENDERER: Frederic Jones, PhD
DESIGNER: Reel/Grobman & Associates

ONE POINT PERSPECTIVE
RENDERED DRAWING
INTRO. TO SPACIAL DEPICTION

LIST OF PLATES

Used with permission of:

Pages 23 and 24
Steelcase Corporation

Page 25
L and B Corporation

Pages 29, 31 and 33
The Pella/Rollscreen Co.

Pages 73, 79, 80, 81, 83, 84, 85, 86, 87, 88, 89
Reproduced from the *Manual of Millwork*
Published by the Woodwork Institute of California

Page 90
Creative Technologies, Inc.

Page 117
AutoDesk Inc.

Page 123, 125, 127, 131
MegaCAD

Pages 198, 199, 200, 201, 202, 203, 204, 205, 206, 207
Western Design Institute
Brigitte Blumberg, Student Project

Pages 208 and 209
Wayne Ruga, Environmental Design
San Francisco, Ca.

Pages 211, 212, 213, 214, 215, 216, 221, 222, 223, 228
Kennedy/Bowen Associates, Inc.
San Francisco, Ca.

Pages 224, 225, 226, 227, 229
Courtesy Watson-Guptill Publications

The Entourage pages are courtesy Professor Edward T. White and Architectural Media, Tuscon, AZ.

Computer Aided Drawing Illustrations as well as software to develop and plot the drawings were provided by Imagimedia Technologies publishers of MicroCad and MegaCAD publishers of Design Board 3D Professional. A DMP-52 plotter was loaned by Houston Instruments. Two dimensional CAD software was provided by AutoDesk Inc. publishers of AutoCAD and Calcomp publishers of CADVANCE.

Unless noted above, all the illustrations in this book are by the author.

BIBLIOGRAPHY

Atkins, William Wilson. *Architectural Presentation Techniques*. New York: Van Nostrand Reinhold, 1976.

Berkeley, George Bishop. *New Theory of Vision*

Burden, Ernest. *Entourage*: *A Tracing File for Architectural and Interior Design Drawing*. New York: McGraw-Hill Paperbacks, 1981.

Ching, Frank. *Architectural Graphics*. New York: Van Nostrand Reinhold, 1975.

Cornsweet, Tom N. *Visual Perception*. New York: Academic Press, 1970.

De Chiara, Joseph. *Handbook of Architectural Details for Commercial Buildings*. New York: McGraw-Hill, Inc., 1980.

Diekman, Norman, and Pile, John. *Drawing Interior Architecture*. New York: Whitney Library of Design, (imprint of Watson-Guptill Publications), 1983.

Gibson, J.J. *The Perception of the Visual World*. Boston: Houghton Mifflin, 1950.

Ittleson, W.H. *Visual Space Perception*. New York: Springer, 1960.

Kaufman, L. *Sight and Mind: an introduction to visual perception*. New York: Oxford University Press, 1974.

Kicklighter, Clois E., and Baird, Ronald J. *Architecture: Residential Drawing and Design.* South Holland (Illinois): The Goodheart-Wilcox Co., 1973.

Olin, Harold B., Schmidt, John L., and Lewis, Walter H. *Construction: Principles, Materials, and Methods.* Chicago: Institute of Financial Education, 1975.

Panero, Jules. *Anatomy for Interior Designers.* New York: Whitney Publishers.

Panero, Jules, and Zelnik, Martin. *Human Dimension and Interior Space.* New York: Whitney Library of Design (imprint of Watson-Guptill Publications), 1979.

Pile, John. *Drawings of Architectural Interiors.* New York: Whitney Library of Design, 1967.

Ramsey, Charles G. and Sleeper, Harold R. *Architectural Graphic Standards*, 8th Edition. New York: John Wiley & Sons, Inc., 1980

Wakita, Osamu A. and Linde, Richard M. *The Professional Practice of Architectural Detailing.* New York: John Wiley and Sons, 1977.

White, Edward T. *A Graphic Vocabulary for Architectural Presentation.* Tuscon: Architectural Media, 1972.

Wyatt, William E. *General Architectural Drawing.* Chas. A. Bennett Co., 1969.

Designed by Frederic Jones